Women Voice Men
Gender in European Culture

Edited by Maya Slater

intellect™

EXETER, ENGLAND

First Published in 1997 by
Intellect Books
EFAE, Earl Richards Road North, Exeter EX2 6AS

Consulting editor: Masoud Yazdani
Copy Editor: Wendy Momen
Cover Design: Amanda Brown
Production Design: Elise Belsher

A catalogue record for this book is available from the British Library

ISBN 1-871516-93-5

Printed and bound in Great Britain by Cromwell Press, Wiltshire

Contents

Introduction

Maya Slater

Women have never been more aware of their position relative to men. Questions of sexual discrimination and sexual prejudice preoccupy us at home, in the workplace, abroad. We are fascinated by the problems women have to face because they are women. This interest can be all-absorbing and, indeed, it dominates the outlook of many women; it also spills over into their attitudes to men. Increasingly, modern thinking women like to approach the other half of humankind from the specific angle of the relationships between the sexes. Partly because the subject of male-female relations is fascinating, partly also because it is fashionable, we are much less likely to look at men without reference to women. To test this idea, I asked a number of modern women writers to produce pieces about men, without specifically inviting them to write about men's attitudes to women. This book is the result.

As I suspected, the relationships between men and women preoccupied all my contributors. Half of them elected to scrutinize men through the eyes of other women writers. The other half focused directly on individual men but chose at some point to examine these men's attitudes to women. My own contribution is no exception: when I decided to look at Proust as a male writer, I found that what I was wanting to write about was his portrayal of a complex and stormy male-female relationship.

The interest in the woman question underlying these essays forms a unifying thread. There is, however, considerable variety in the choice of topic. The men under scrutiny may be writers, politicians or libertines; and their lives as well as their work come under observation. The settings can be stormy. Some of the people examined here lived through the first, others the second World War. There are subtle differences between the nations – for instance, women living in France just before the second war are strongly influenced by the fact that they have only recently acquired the vote, whereas their British counterparts, born entitled to it, can afford to be more rebellious and more outspoken in their criticism of men; a comparison of Jefferson's and Maslen's essays brings this out. But such differences are not clear-cut; we can detect the traces of constant cross-fertilization between the different countries of Europe. So Jane Austen, the subject of a study in her own right by Hobson, also makes an impact, translated, on the French women writers discussed by Finch; and Proust's outlook on women, examined in my own contribution, probably owes much to Freud. The earliest subject, the 18th century statesman Lord Chesterfield evoked by Karsky, is imbued with French culture. And even the most apparently xenophobic subject, Evelyn Waugh, is glimpsed in Pasternak Slater's study revelling in the delights of French North Africa with almost as much gusto as André Gide in Segal's account. And topics of European – and indeed transcontinental – importance were tackled, for instance in the work of Claire de Duras, discussed by Finch, who took as her starting point the publicity about the slave trade early in the 19th century.

The contributions that deal with most recent events are, curiously, the least international. Joannou's essay on Dennis Potter brings home the difference between British and European television before focusing on Potter himself; Shiach's study of recent feminist detective fiction carries few echoes of the European equivalent, which has yet to develop to the same degree; and Maclean's analysis of the present state of matrimonial law demonstrates a very different situation in Britain from the rest of Europe. In this age of mass communication across Europe, it is intriguing to note how popular culture as well as the law have retained their autonomy.

Although these essays do fit into certain patterns as I have suggested, they are strikingly individual. They have been classified in a roughly chronological order.

The first subject is an 18th century politician. The standpoint from which Karsky views her male object of scrutiny is discreetly impartial, although women among Chesterfield's own contemporaries were outraged by Chesterfield's misogyny. Karsky summarizes the content of a collection of letters in which Chesterfield advocates to his son a combination of patrician *sang froid* and dissolute self-indulgence in his dealings with women. She comments that in addition, viewed from the outside, Chesterfield behaved very badly towards women. However, Karsky herself favours a more indulgent view of this wanton peer: the women in his life, downtrodden perhaps, nevertheless spoke of him with affection. Karsky comments acutely: 'Criticism from outside the family cannot always elucidate the strange intimacies of a couple.'

Hobson's essay on Jane Austen also adopts an historical perspective. Writing almost 200 years ago, Austen's complex approach to her male characters tends to be misjudged by modern critics. In particular, Hobson focuses on Mr Knightley in *Emma*. He is traditionally taken as the benchmark of how wrong Emma is in her view of things but this approach undervalues the diversity and irony in Austen's writing. Far from setting up her hero as a model of perfection, Austen views the whole community with irony and also with a wider frame of reference than has been attributed to her. She is far more interested in the comic potential of discourse, both of male and female characters, than in holding a male figure up for the reader's admiration.

But the early 19th-century French women writers in Finch's essay do stress the high status of men. Finch examines the idea of rank in some key works and shows how their authors associate – implicitly or explicitly – the state of being a man with high social status and the state of being a woman with low status. This presentation is interwoven with the rebellion against arranged marriage. The influence of these women will take on a new force in the immediate aftermath of the French Revolution and helps to shape the rhetoric of mid-century Utopian socialists, as well as exerting an influence on later French male writers who are apparently misogynist.

The early years of our century are represented by essays on the two greatest French writers of the time. First we have Segal's piece on Gide. It is composed with a certain degree of anger and much greater puzzlement – anger as a modern feminist confronting the entrenched superiority of a male writer of 50 years ago; puzzlement as to what standpoint a feminist writer should adopt vis-à-vis a gay male writer, who earns her respect by his honesty but forfeits it by his misogyny and pederasty. In her essay, critic and subject are viewed as equals. She demonstrates how the personality and the attitudes of the modern feminist writer have as much right to be examined as the pronouncements of the 'canonical' literary figure. The process she is describing is a pact between writer and reader – but in this case, a reader who feels unwanted by the writer.

My own contribution focuses on the in-depth psychology of the first great introspective self-analyst novelist, Marcel Proust. I examine the negative attitude to women and love in that most misogynistic of characters, the Narrator of Proust's *Remembrance of Things Past*. Reading between the lines, I detect a self-destructive urge in the character, of which he himself seems unaware: he manipulates his relationship with Albertine so as to make it impossible for her to love him. He does this because of his conviction that she stays with him through self-interest, not love; but that is an assumption that is largely contradicted by the facts. I focus exclusively on Proust's character as opposed to his life, detecting complex and often self-contradictory urges within him.

The First World War was a watershed – during it, for the first time, women could participate fully in independent, active life. Between the two wars, they felt uneasy with their situation, as Maslen's study shows. From an historical perspective, she examines the approach of a group of intelligent, articulate women between the wars towards their menfolk. Their stance evokes mingled admiration for their forbearance, compassion for their plight and horror at the positions they were forced to adopt. While some of them seem too ready to acquiesce in their relegation by men to second place, others are well aware of the injustice of their lot. These are the women who clearly feel that their position needs clarification, hence the tenor of their contributions to the volume of their essays discussed here, which appeared in 1932. Storm Jameson sums up the position of her more militant contemporaries when she laments that women must 'keep silent, with itching fingers, while man bungles the tasks she can do. . .supremely well'. Other women give up on men in disgust, like Rebecca West, who comments: 'The masculine temperament. . .tends towards repulsive excess.'

In her examination of Evelyn Waugh, who wrote much of his fiction during and after the ordeal of the second World War, Ann Pasternak Slater rejects attempts to categorize the writer as 'the archetypal male chauvinist pig'. She argues that his writing, and his life, are much more complex and *nuancé* than this. Evelyn Waugh is in particular danger of being treated as a misogynist, since his stance is provocative and satirical. However, Pasternak Slater points out that it is impossible to go along with this view of him without omitting important material, both in his works and in his life, which suggests the opposite. The implication of her argument is that it is not acceptable for the critic to pigeonhole another human being and then to set aside the aspects of his life and work that fail to fit.

Nathalie Sarraute's long life spans most of our century. Jefferson demonstrates that to Sarraute the position of the woman writer (a label she herself rejects) is impossible without input from men. This is the case both within her novels (in which she tries to identify with male characters and to put them across to the reader), and with the reception of her works by the public. A profoundly contradictory situation arises, in which the woman writer has to use her femininity to gain acceptance into the ostensibly asexual world of letters. Ultimately, she achieves recognition as a writer by seeking endorsement from men like her contemporary Sartre. With their backing, she can make her way in the world.

But whereas novelists have struggled for generations to make their voices heard impartially whatever their sex, the same cannot be said for the newer medium of television. Joannou gives us a feminist reading of Dennis Potter, whose work makes her angry. But before she even gets to Potter himself, she detects a problem for women in TV in general. She writes: 'Much of television has assumed the male point of view to be normative and has taken women and images of women as its object of scrutiny; it has seldom investigated men and the male image in the same way.' Potter adopts the male viewpoint wholeheartedly, but the reverence that surrounds his undoubtedly innovative and impressive output, especially since his death, has prevented critics from confronting this problem in his work. Joannou unpicks *The Singing Detective* from this angle, detecting behind the modish and lively surface the author's undoubted misogyny. Women may well feel uncomfortable with Potter's work; Joannou shows us why – the whole saga is the story of the hero's attempt to impose some sort of order on female sexuality, which he finds deeply disturbing.

The feminist detective-story writers analysed by Shiach are in some ways tackling the same sort of problem. Indeed, one of the most curious aspects of this area of fiction is the way these women writers deal with their heroines' sexuality. The women need a particular type of man, 'less erotic than cuddly'. With uncanny similarity, each of the male partners is fitted into a pattern. He is divorced (hence capable of long-term relationships, albeit with an ultimate element of failure). He is the (part-time) father of a son (so the heroine does not have to cope with the more problematic mother-daughter relationship). The lifestyles of the couple are at least partly separate. The genre of feminist detective writing will come of age when the women described are able to enter into other, less restricted, permutations.

It is not easy to portray women in fiction as fully in command when they continue to be disadvantaged in their lives. Maclean's essay, which concludes the book, shows that in terms of legal rights we still have far to go. A sociologist and lawyer, she is exercised by the extent to which divorce law reforms, formulated to make the situation fairer for women, actually do the opposite. Maclean's solution, which seems to be the only practical one, could be described as radically anti-feminist: she thinks women would be less disadvantaged if the ongoing family unit were better protected. Ostensibly 'fairer' solutions drastically penalize women, since we are automatically disadvantaged by being the child-bearers and suffer financially as a result, since child-bearing (and child-rearing while we continue to take responsibility for it) erodes our earning capacity and pension entitlement.

Despite the variety of tone and subject-matter in this collection, the contributors share the same underlying values. All share a desire for fair treatment of women which informs their arguments. It may cause them to defend the men they are discussing, if, like Pasternak Slater or Karsky, they feel that their particular subject has not been as misogynistic as others might assume. It may lead them to attack, 'we the hunters, they the prey', as Segal puts it. They can feel sympathy for the straight-jacketed role of their predecessors (Maslen) or angry at the position they are put in today (Joannou). Whatever their stance, the women writing in this collection are not content just to talk about men. What really exercises them is the interaction between men and women; and on the whole, they feel that there is still much to be said and done on this subject.

Revisiting Chesterfield: Gender and Courtesy in the Eighteenth Century

Barbara Karsky

In 1779 Mercy Otis Warren wrote to her son Winslow, who was contemplating touring Europe: 'I perceive. . . you are enraptured with Lord Chesterfield, nor do I wonder at it. . . This masterly writer has furnished the present generation with a code of politeness, which, perhaps, surpasses anything of the kind in the English language.' She admired Chesterfield's style and expression, his knowledge of the 'arts of life' and what she called his 'complete system of refinement' before warning her son not to confuse Chesterfield the author with Chesterfield the man. The letter goes on to oppose the values of republican womanhood to those of monarchical masculinity.

Warren's criticisms were aimed essentially at what she considered to be Chesterfield's immorality: insincerity, lack of true sentiment, the sacrifice of higher values to expediency, licentious provocation, and finally, contemptuous misogyny. In this mother's epistle to her son, which begins on a tone of admiration for the 'elegant diction' and 'thousand beauties of expression' of a 'masterly writer', our English lord is rapidly transformed into a sort of diabolic figure whose 'cloven step' leads the novitiate son (hers, she fears, as well as his) into 'every species of vice'. Whether her son obliged with a 'generous, resolute, manly fortitude' and resisted the temptations of vice differently than did Chesterfield's son in response to his father's urgings towards gallantry, is a moot question. In both cases, it is the parental correspondence which carries historical weight. Each wrote in a society where letters were shared and circulated. Mercy Otis Warren's judgement of Chesterfield as an 'accomplish'd debauchee' resonated favourably in a country struggling for independence. Her letter was soon taken up by Abigail Adams and sent to Boston's *Independent Chronicle* for publication. First printed in January 1781, it was twice reprinted in New England periodicals within the decade.[1]

Who was this Chesterfield who moved Warren to write with such feeling to her son and who inflamed American women's tempers to the point of disseminating her counsels in the press? Everyone knows something about Chesterfield and yet we know him little. Frequently cited or alluded to in reference to the history of manners, he is not infrequently misconstrued. Despite a rather hostile reception to his *Letters to His Son* when it was first published in London in 1774, the numerous editions and translations appearing before the end of the century attest to its popularity. Nor did public eagerness to read the letters diminish. Several more editions had appeared by the early

1800s and a Japanese translation offered Chesterfield to a still larger public by the late 19th century. Over time, his advice has truly become 'worldly', as readers continue to consult popular hardback editions and paperback versions even in the 1990s.

The 4th Earl of Chesterfield, Philip Dormer Stanhope – born and died in London (1694–1773) – came into the world in the same year as Voltaire, with whom he shared affinities. The eldest of six, Stanhope was brought up with his sister Gertrude in the house of their maternal grandmother, Lady Halifax. There they were sheltered from the vicissitudes of their mother's unhappy marriage to the 2nd Earl of Chesterfield, who regarded his children with antipathy. Bred for the world of the Court, brother and sister were introduced to London society in the Halifax home, where they received a bilingual education from English governesses and French tutors. Philip spent a year at Trinity College Cambridge before travelling on the continent and in 1715 was named Gentleman of the Bedchamber to the Prince of Wales. From then on his life was defined by the seats of power and its course vacillated between Parliament and foreign embassies, alternating with moments of idleness when he was in royal or ministerial disfavour. On the death of his father in 1726, he became the 4th Earl of Chesterfield.

Appointed Ambassador to the Hague and invested with the Garter, Chesterfield's hostility to Walpole's fiscal policies in the early 1730s placed him in the ranks of the opposition where he remained for the rest of his political career, serving as Lord Lieutenant of Ireland in 1745, then as Secretary of State until his resignation in 1748.

While Ambassador at the Hague, Chesterfield met Elizabeth du Bouchet, governess or companion in a Dutch family; she bore him a son in 1732. Chesterfield brought 'la Bouchet' to London and set up his little family in separate lodgings, where his son was surrounded by governesses and French tutors, as he himself had been. The following year, at 39, he married a woman of about the same age, the Countess of Walsingham, Melusina de Schulumbergh, natural daughter of George I by the Duchess of Kendal. Chesterfield confided to friends before his marriage that he wanted a wealthy woman of a placid nature whose fortune could help alleviate his debts and support his son and concubine. They were said to have lived amiably in neighbouring houses in Grosvenor Square until the death of his mother-in-law.[2] In the meantime and for many years London gossips observed Lady Frances Shirley on the arm of Lord Chesterfield at any significant social event.

Chesterfield moved in various circles – that of the Court and its fringes, the world of letters, the clubs and gaming houses, and the Masonic Order. His tastes and his acquaintances extended to Parisian salons and to the courts of the Low Countries and Prussia, where his wit and statesmanship were appreciated by Frederick the Great. He admired and was admired by Pope, Montesquieu and Voltaire. Known by contemporaries for the poems, essays and character studies he contributed to London literary journals, his lasting reputation rests on his letters.

Those to his son begin in 1737, when the boy was five, and continue until the young man's death in 1768. Those to his godson and heir (born in 1755) extend from 1761 to Chesterfield's own death in 1773. A few of the latter were published in serial form in the *Edinburgh Magazine and Review* in 1774, but Chesterfield's advice and what we know of his personality have come down to us especially through the letters to his son.

A content analysis of these letters brings three major themes to the fore: first learning, next the importance of good breeding and grace, and finally women in their various relations to polite society. On all of these points Chesterfield has much to say, and they recur at frequent intervals throughout the correspondence, although he devotes more attention to the theme of education in his son's youth and introduces the others in his adolescent years.

Chesterfield begins to stress concentration and attentiveness when his son Philip is seven, urging him to think about what he is doing, whether at work or at play. He tells him at age nine that lack of attention means lack of thought – and, the following year, that only through attention can one excel. Gradually the emphasis shifts from formal learning to behaviour – look someone in the face when speaking, be present when listening – and eventually to attention to character: observe, not only people's manners, but 'go deeper still; observe their characters, and pry as far as you can, into both their hearts and their heads'.[3]

Such advice corresponds to Chesterfield's belief that the knowledge of man is more important than book-learning. Chesterfield frequently recommends authors to his son – among the classics Cicero, Virgil and Ovid. But, characteristic of liberal thinkers in the Enlightenment, his tastes run to the modern – to Dryden, Pope and Swift among his compatriots, and in French literature to La Rochefoucauld, La Bruyère and especially Voltaire. He advises the 14-year-old Philip to hoard knowledge while young, for it will stand him in good stead in later life, but also suggests that books alone are inadequate teachers. He warns him against bibliomania and pedantry, the bane of polite society. Chesterfield's goal in educating his son is to unite the scholar with the courtier, a union which he feels is rare among Englishmen. For this, he writes, one must know oneself and know others – and that demands attention.[4]

More ink is spent on reflecting upon good-breeding and manners than on formal learning. In this domain Chesterfield esteems that the influence of women is important. When Philip was young, Chesterfield recommended his reading the Marquise de Lambert's *Advice to her Son* which stressed the study of human nature and the importance of pleasing. Later, he repeatedly hinted that a relationship with an older woman would help round off the rough edges of his son's character.

When his letters were published, such suggestions offended the sentiments of many of his readers, especially in the immediate aftermath of Wesley's preachings. Chesterfield became, in Cowper's lines, the 'Greybeard corrupter of our listening youth'.[5] But as Richard Bushman points out in his study of courtesy literature, each time a book of etiquette appeared, it was challenged, mocked and satirized and its readers warned against the 'dangers of court life'.[6] Chesterfield had been formed in the Augustan Age and found good sense in Mme de Lambert's admission to her son that good breeding served as a veil for vice at court. Her *Advice to her Daughter* taught another lesson, however – that good-breeding is nothing without merit, an admonition which echoed the double standards of *ancien régime* morality and reconfirmed the gender divisions of its society. Chesterfield's own mother had received similar advice in 1688 from her father, George Savile, Marquis of Halifax, whose counsel, published under the title *The Lady's New-Year's Gift; or, Advice to a Daughter* would spread as far as the American colonies.[7]

Good breeding was a much-discussed concept, variously defined by Locke, Swift and others. Swift distinguished between good manners, which he defined as 'the Art of making those people easy with whom we converse', and good breeding, the latter encompassing a wide range of knowledge and necessitating much study and labour to acquire.[8] Repeatedly, Chesterfield entreated his son to study others and learn the graces, to obtain those 'shining' qualities which enhance all social contact. Breeding was based on good sense, while good manners were the 'cement and security' of society. Their attainment demanded discipline and self-control, which Chesterfield made the habit of a lifetime.

An element of this restraint was the separation of the public and the private, or personal, parts of one's life. In conversation, for instance, he advises his son not to talk of himself; that would be boorish. This consideration was widely accepted in the mid-18th century. Chesterfield's contemporary, Lady Mary Montagu, declared: 'fig-leaves are as necessary for our minds as our bodies, and 'tis as indecent to show all we think as all we have'.[9] This type of thinking was challenged in the last quarter of the century when an emphasis on 'sincerity' confused prudence with dissimulation of the truth. On both sides of the Atlantic Chesterfield's precepts were castigated as self-interested and deceitful, but, as a recent scholar points out, this insistence on frankness could turn against itself. In assuming that the 'hidden is the "real"' it encouraged the development of cynicism. [10] Read as a key to success, Chesterfield's letters were very often meant rather to teach his son how to avoid ridicule and social pain, how not to be vulnerable, how to survive.

Chesterfield's reflections on women show little of the rational influences of Enlightenment thinking. Although he admired the letters of Mme de Lambert and of Mme de Sévigné, and often recommended certain Continental acquaintances to his son for their refinement and conversation (finding Englishwomen dull and silent in comparison), he seemed to think of them merely as vehicles to success and considered them like large children.

It is difficult to ascertain the role of women in Chesterfield's life. His mother, as direct recipient of Halifax's oppressive (but for the period standard) counsel, could have been a symbol of submissiveness, but her headstrong behaviour proved her otherwise. Certainly her unhappy marriage, the misfortunes she suffered from a 'sour' husband, and her quasi-abandonment of Chesterfield and his sister Gertrude, must have engendered ambiguous feelings in him about women and marriage. It is equally difficult to know the importance that either wife or mistress had for him; they only appear sporadically in the *Letters*, and these would hardly be a vehicle of expression for his feelings towards either. We do know that Lady Chesterfield accepted both her husband's natural son and the boy's mother in her home and interested herself in Philip's progress in German. Occasional letters from sympathetic friends remonstrate against Chesterfield's apparent lack of consideration for her in gadding about with Lady Frances Shirley. When his will was published Chesterfield was strongly criticized for his stinginess towards her. However, criticism from outside the family cannot always elucidate the strange intimacies of a couple. Whatever society said about their relationship, Lady Chesterfield wrote respectfully and tenderly about her husband after his death. Chesterfield's comments to his son on the importance of good breeding as a regulator of social relations are a precious key to his own views on marriage:

The most familiar and intimate habitudes, connections and friendships, require a degree of good-breeding, both to preserve and cement them. If ever a man and his wife, or a man and his mistress, who pass nights as well as days together, absolutely lay aside all good-breeding, their intimacy will soon degenerate into a coarse familiarity, infallibly productive of contempt or disgust. The best of us have our bad sides and it is as imprudent as it is ill-bred to exhibit them. [11]

The woman who ultimately played a significant role in Chesterfield's future was his daughter-in-law, Eugenia Stanhope. It was from her hand that he learned of the death of his son in 1768 and simultaneously of his secret marriage and the existence of two grandsons. Chesterfield concealed whatever shock he felt at these discoveries and welcomed them all into his home. Upon his death, the boys were provided for in his will, but not the daughter-in-law. She, however, provided for herself by publishing the correspondence of Lord Chesterfield to his son. Her ungenteel action, condemned by the Stanhope family, permitted an Oxford education for the boys and an annuity for her own lifetime – and ensured a permanent name for Chesterfield in history.

In his active life, Chesterfield seems to demonstrate what Anthony Fletcher describes as the masculinity of the 18th century – 'cerebral and bloodless'.[12] In the *Letters*, he advocates a model of rational self-discipline which he hopes his son will achieve. Yet gradually, beneath his reserve, his humanity unfolds. His sentiments, like that of his period, 'must be read between the lines. . . "True elegance appears with mild restraint/Decent, discreet, and proper, yet not quaint"'.[13]

Not a woman-friendly man, the Chesterfield of the *Letters* is nevertheless an endearing figure, whose attitude towards his son shows a touching fidelity which transcends the son's failure to meet his father's goals in public and private life. Augustan by the timing of his birth and education, by his interests a man of the Enlightenment, Chesterfield in his frank observations of people in society was, and remains for us today, a vivid example of a man of all times.

1. Hayes, Edmund M. 'Mercy Otis Warren versus Lord Chesterfield, 1779'. *William and Mary Quarterly,* 3rd series, vol. 40, n. 3 (Oct. 1983), pp. 616-21.
2. Lucas, F.L. *The Search for Good Sense*. N.Y. Macmillan, 1958, p. 133.
3. Letter of 5 Sept. 1748, in Lord Chesterfield *Letters* ed. David Roberts. Oxford University Press, 1992.
4. Letters of 5 Sept. 1748, 23 Jan. and 4 Oct. 1752. *ibid.*
5. Letters of 5 Sept. 1748, 23 Jan. and 4 Oct. 1752. *ibid.*
6. Bushman, Richard L. *The Refinement of America, Persons, Houses, Cities*. N.Y. Alfred A. Knopf, 1992, p. 60.
7. Mason, John Edward. *Gentlefolk in the Making: Studies in the History of English Courtesy Literature and Related Topics from 1531 to 1774*. N.Y. Octagon, 1971 (1st ed. 1935), p. 94.
8. Swift, Jonathan. *A Treatise on Good-Manners and Good-Breeding*, in Horn, Colin J., ed., *Swift on his Age*, London. Harrap. 1953, p. 70.
9. Gay, Peter. *The Enlightenment: an Interpretation*. vol. 2: *The Science of Freedom*. N.Y. : Alfred A. Knopf, 1966-9, p. 202.

10. Fliegelman, Jay. *Declaring Independence: Jefferson, Natura l Language & the Culture of Performance.* Stanford, CA: Stanford University Press, 1993, p. 123.
11. Letter of November 3, 1749, *op. cit.,* p. 169.
12. Fletcher, Anthony. *Gender, Sex & Subordination in England, 1500-1800.* New Haven, CT: Yale University Press, 1985, p. 338.
13. Dobrée, Bonamy. *The Early Eighteenth Century, 1700-1740.* Oxford: Clarendon Press, 1990, p. 223.

Knightley as a Screen near Us

Marian Hobson

Jane Austen's defended moderation in self-regard and appetite for influence (Chapman, 1952, letter 126) is at variance with the torsion her work has undergone nearly two hundred years later: a huge financial success through film, bought by procrustean adjustments to plot and tone; a peculiar institutionalisation of her name in the contemporary canon made possible, but also paid for, by too etiolated a celebration of the 'great tradition'. As it is, film producers and Austenian criticism may have more in common than might appear.

By English critics (much less by Americans), the novels are seen as ideological: they are said to espouse a moral code, belonging to the gentry. And, no doubt, they do. But not just, or solely, or even, in the case of *Emma*, mainly. The extent of this engagement by critics may go largely unmentioned and that it is itself ideological is infrequently recognized. At the heart of this problem is the question of Austen's relation to the satirical tradition: 'It is hard to think of another major novelist whose diction provides, to a comparable extent, a key to the qualities held to be desirable, and ultimately, to the moral attitudes behind the novels. (Perhaps Fielding provides one of the few comparable instances.)' (Page, 1972, 55). Or again, 'the firmness and precision of the words used are a token of the clear and unambiguous standards by which human behaviour is assessed. *For ambiguity may serve as a valuable source of comedy*, but the moral basis of the author's judgements, conveyed in her language, finds modes of expression which leave us in no doubt as to her standpoint' (Page, 1972, 47-8, my italics). That the 18th and early 19th centuries, European and English, used language to delineate moral qualities in an absolute way is evident – compare the distinctions made available in such a vulgar Lavaterian treatise as *Les sympathies, ou l'art de juger par les traits du visage, des convenances en amour et en amité* (Paris, 1813) for instance, or the much more fine grained though often lapidary moral evaluations in Constant's *Adolphe*. But one might wish, in regard to Fielding as well as Austen, not to identify inevitably and everywhere the sententiousness of the style with an indubitable meaning, to acknowledge a complexity from effects of writing which is not morally *ambiguous*, but not with a presented moral absolute either. Eighteenth century assuredness in writing may do work for irony. Or, differently, sententiousness may gather into a momentary oracular brilliance, sometimes both pithy and ponderous, which allows an unexpected irony to appear (and in that way is quite different from 19th century effects). It is as if at times in Austen the same processes are at work but more muted, fluent, less attention seeking. In *Emma*, particularly, the narrative's poise in judgement is as much linguistic as moral; it operates as a perturbable irony to register slight destabilisings, allowing a humour which is almost without contrast, almost flat.

With other critics, their own commitment is more conscious. In a fine article, Graham Hough, for instance, considers the novels 'as strongly ideological constructions. They are recommendations to regard society and experience in a certain way; they are powerful reinforcements of a particular class structure and of a moral structure adapted to support it' (Hough, 1970, 200). One of the few moral stands indisputably present in all the novels, the strong dislike of class snobbery, visible from *Pride and Prejudice* (Darcy escapes, but only just) to the first paragraph of *Persuasion*, is inverted by Hough to become 'a refusal to entertain the possibilities of class ideologies, the acceptance of the values of the upper bourgeoisie as non-historical absolutes' (Hough, 1970, 201). Hough's Austen helped, we are told, to create a strand which, while contributing to the stability of British politics, has cut British culture off from the continent, and from history. His quasi-Marxist stance does indeed point to what her novels have become with us; but it is part of that very tradition of reading which has narrowed them more than necessary.

Marilyn Butler, in the magisterial *Jane Austen and the War of Idea*, related the novels not to 20th century ideology but to that of the beginning 19th: she considered the options in writing that Austen did not choose, what the plots and incidents of the novels suggest of her resistance to those tendencies in the culture around her which encouraged expression of sensibility and individual assertion without respect of the social unit. The code of behaviour which her preferred characters adopt is thus not universal but participates in a conservative reaction (Butler, 1975, xv). In the novels, what has come among feminists to be referred to as 'the marriage plot' is crucial as a system of reward for moral development. It is true that in the preface to the second edition of her book, Butler accepted that the theme of social integration through marriage is less marked in the final novels than she had previously argued. (Indeed, the first interpretation of the final novel was only possible by separating the narrative focus, Anne Elliot, from the moral one, said to be Frederick Wentworth, thus it seems to me neglecting both the title and the comparison in the novel of two forms of courage; omitting moreover the foundations of Wentworth's fortune – permitted naval piracy, the 'prize system', not land; at the end Anne has confirmed socially by marriage the moral separation from her eldest sister and father which existed at the beginning, and there is no talk of the Wentworths rescuing Kellynch Hall from any creditors who may lie in wait.)

The view that Austen is 'building up a scale . . . for the proper conduct of the moral life' (Bradbury, 1962, 157) is shared by many, probably most, critics. But in this way, the novels are turned into enormously intelligent conduct books, the proof that they were so intended lying for most critics in the successful marriage that is their outcome – the marriage is the prize which rewards improvement in character or discernment (Bradbury, 1962, 157). A more exalted version, then, of the cinema's, where the novels are romantic fiction clad in Quality Street costumes, of a piece with their distant progeniture, the tales of Georgette Heyer, in which the heroine gets the right man. This explains at bargain basement level the strange public status of the novels, their crucial contribution to the forming of the imagination of British women (see the confessions in the newspapers during the height of the filmic triumphs in the winter 1995-6); and in more exciting and ambitious fashion, where the novels are held to promulgate the values of the late-18th century English gentry, and to be distinct in scale and social views from continental trends (in reaction to political movements associated with Europe), this is one more symptom of the particularity, or insularity, of the tradition of English fiction.

The following is an essay in exorcism. Austen may, by virtue of her place and time, be working within a wider European tradition, one to which some, though not all, of the writers whose style she developed, Fielding and Sterne also belonged (not, perhaps, Richardson). Ezra Pound in this vein pointed to Prévost as precursor and *Adolphe* as contemporary, all three seen as opening the way for Stendhal (courteously Pound 31, grudgingly 385). Both are sententious – as indeed was the culture of the time. Where *Adolphe* is tragic, Austen is funny. But with such a novel, *Emma* has more than a little in common: a theme of lack of understanding, as owing partly to the necessarily misleading nature of language; sententious expression in a narrative rendered unstable by its very complexity and intelligence. *Emma* has been flattened out by our critical tradition's attitude to language; though Park Honan has reminded us of all that Austen owes to Sterne (Honan, 1984), most critics would seem to share Page's insistent turning from the force of the style to the characterizing meaning to be attributed to it. It is as characterizing, whether of people or relationships (see for example the exchange about the snow between Emma and Knightley, Butler, 1975, 265) that language must function.

It is in the writing of little things that one may show that *Emma* goes beyond even a very complex system of imagined referents. The deliberate triviality of the events has occasioned much comment. Yet the stylization of this triviality has not really been discussed, nor its connection with language, as far as I can see, except in relation to Mr Cole's party, where it is clearly thematized: 'the usual rate of conversation; a few clever things said, a few downright silly, but by much the larger proportion neither the one nor the other – nothing worse than everyday remarks, dull repetitions, old news and heavy jokes' (*Emma*, 219). Likewise, attention to Mr Knightley's declaration of love – in a very funny scene which works through but by no means lifts a series of considerable misunderstandings, and which acknowledges that 'seldom, very seldom, does complete truth belong to any human disclosure; seldom can it happen that something is not a little disguised or a little mistaken' – backing this up by just such a distinction between feelings and conduct as is condemned apparently in *Sense and Sensibility* – tends to be allocated to poststructuralist critics (Lodge, 23) rather than to any treatment of the theme of disclosure within a structure of closure. All this comes to a visible head in the treatment of Mr Knightly himself.

The marriage plot is often taken at romantic value, with the financial aspect glossed over. Knightley has 'little spare money' and so does not much use his carriage; the Woodhouses on the other hand are *rentiers*, though established in Highbury for several generations (MacDonagh, 1991). Land marries wealth in this novel (Emma is worth £30,000, Darcy's sister's fortune). But in a sense, however minute the finances in the novel are – and they are quite minute, once one starts looking – such glossings-over are right. This is not a novel about money; the financial motive for the final marriage is not even mooted (unlike *Pride and Prejudice*). So a kind of moral romanticism intervenes: Knightley, even in the very brilliant interpretation of Marilyn Butler, represents the right view (254 note). He is 'never wrong' (Hough, 190). (Feminist disculpations of Emma must consequently involve trying, against the weight of the evidence, to place doubt on his actions.) He is, rightly, recognized as the view against which Emma's mistakes of judgement can be hinted at (he begins, for instance, to suspect the private understanding existing between the two quasi-adopted children who come into the world of Highbury, Jane Fairfax and Frank Churchill).

This function in the novel becomes in much criticism a moral one: the incarnation of attitudes to land and wealth, and of the virtues of cool judgement and thought for others, the bench mark against which the other characters may be measured. This 'corrective' view, then (the word is Bradbury's), is not the point of view from which the novel is written[1] (Booth), and the separation is sustained, for we only see him in more interior fashion once or twice in relation to Jane Fairfax's symptoms of private understanding with Churchill, before the end, where there is some insight into his feelings for Emma (the paragraph beginning 'he had, in fact, been wholly unsuspicious of his own influence', *Emma*, 432, being in *style indirect libre*). Unlike Darcy or Frederick Wentworth, he doesn't seem to develop, unless it is in his recognition that he is in love, and we barely see that. Unlike Colonel Brandon in *Sense and Sensibility*, he doesn't have an amorous past, although he is seven or eight and thirty. We are given little material for Emma-style speculation on his account – biographically he is extremely thin. His service as screen onto which values may be projected is the easier: values claimed as those of the English landed gentry, as Page does; or part of the shift of attitude which made possible the Reform Act (as I would tend to do – of Robert Martin's rank in society he says 'I would alter [it] if I could, which is saying a great deal, I assure you' *Emma*, 472-3).'

For in spite of the hints as to the financial situations of the novel, and possible speculation as to his politics (compare Darcy, or Sir Walter Elliot – Mr Knightley does not merely act on the Parish Council with Mr Cole and Mr Elton, he dines with them[2]), he is the unequivocal sign of the highly stylized nature of this novel. *Emma* is a kind of idyll (Trilling, 1957): nothing very much goes wrong (compare the other novels – adultery, heart-break, illness, depression) and it ends happily. But it is an idyll of a modern kind. The intensely ordinary is uniquely conventionalised, the boring and trite are held up for amused inspection in a way which, without contrast – the brilliance is disguised – uses techniques prefiguring Bakhtin's typology of discourse in prose (in Matejka and Pomorska, 1971). This typology is developed in his book on Dostoievsky, whose central purpose is to suggest a connection between the history of the novel and 'dialogism', that is a narrative system of independent 'voices' or better, discursive centres. I shall merely point out here that the four elements

Bakhtin isolates (which he designates as a heritage from Fielding and Sterne) must prevent any too literal interpretation of *Emma*'s plot and univocalising of the novel's language. Stylisation, dialogue, parody and 'skaz' (an untranslatable term, to be explained later) are all here, in a manner which enjoys this kind double orientation of language but which also does not leave it as 'mere play' – its relation to a dark side of experience is hinted at in different ways which will be broached at the end of this article. The critical fear of the sign which has almost cut loose from any meaning of weight, if not from its referent, breathes then occasionally in this novel, a mortal breath but not unsurprising if Derrida is right to connect such fear with fear of death and if, as I surmise, Austen's illness was already upon her.

The very considerable stylisation through names and plot has in part a theatrical ancestry, it seems to me. Knightley's name has often been remarked on. He is not on the same existential footing as the others, and yet with Austen's powers of imagination, the stylisation does not make him seem empty. He comes from and goes back to cool masterful seclusion, his home Donwell Abbey; his acolytes are both bird names, Robert Martin, William Larkins; he meets his love at Hart – field. The name Woodhouse, on the contrary, although in Emma's meditation on Mr Elton's pretensions we are told that they were 'the younger branch of a very ancient family', suggests to me lack of nobility; it certainly indicates the impermanence of semi-camping.

The stylisation is even more important in the marriage plot – as indeed it is in the plot of several Austen novels. The pattern whereby the heroine finds out whom it is she wishes to marry reminds of Marivaux and his emulators (even if, as seems likely, Austen knew neither his plays nor his narratives).[3] The development, sometimes of a woman, sometimes of a couple, through obstacles to understanding which are largely internal, are in both *oeuvres* an important shape of plot. In both, the certainty that there will be marriage is what enables closure and what makes possible our amused concentration on the emotional and moral development leading to that closure. In *Emma*, there is surprise about whom Emma will actually marry, and this surprise, coupled with the secret of the Fairfax-Churchill engagement, is necessary to provide tension; for Austen plays in a truly breathtaking way with boredom, actual with the heroine, potential with the reader. There is, of course, moral meaning attached to this closure, just as there are realistic finances, but the tendency of critics, especially feminist ones, to neglect just how important is its stylisation, leads precisely to taking the projections onto the screen that is Knightley for real. In their anxiety to denounce apparent deference on the part of the heroine to a strong-minded man, often of higher social class, they forget that Austen in her life did not marry and that that was a conscious, though no doubt difficult, choice (that seems to be about all that is known of the acceptance and then rejection of the rich Bigg Wither's offer). Recognition of the degree of deliberate stylisation in the novel is important because it leads otherwise to such statements as 'the structure of *Emma* is not at all like the structure of the real world' (Hough, 194) (in spite of Mr Knightley's thick leather gaiters). In fact, the highly formal quality of all her plots has to be built into interpretation, so that the weddings become, as they are in Shakespeare's comedies, creation of a new family unit, festivity, closure, licence to laugh and be happy, for all will be well. The world may not be like this, but comic art often is.

In *Emma*, Austen uses a plot form that goes back to *Don Quixote* and which will in the 19th century be worked on by Flaubert in *Madame Bovary* as it was in the 18th by many novelists both English and French. The misapprehensions about reality (caused usually, but not in *Emma*, by reading too many novels) are placed against a ground of often vulgar or common-place events; novelists such as Marivaux examine the status of imaginative experience (Hobson, 1982). One of the interesting technical innovations in Austen's novel is that the heroine's imaginings are based on facts which are themselves novelish – Mr Dixon has saved Jane Fairfax from drowning, as Frank Churchill saves Harriet from the gypsies. If these imaginings are continuations of the novelish quality of the 'actual' event, they are also presented in the first case as more vulgar in their insistent conjectures about feelings than that 'actuality' could be. Yet although Austen makes these imaginings slightly prurient, she places the misjudgments against a 'reality' in the novel which is as damaging to the objects, whether they be Fairfax, Churchill or Elton, as Emma's fancy, but a 'reality' judged by a character who, while he has the traditional debunking function, is also ideal. Knightley has then the role of the practical foil, against which these imaginings show up, but, in another technical innovation, this foil is a Mentor figure (from Fénélon's *Télémaque*).[4] The comparison necessary to satire is thus obtained without the wilful down-to-earthness of Flaubert and sometimes of Fielding. It can be mild without being slight, sustained without being obtrusive.

The degree to which the novel consists of dialogue has excited much comment and forms a central point of attention in Hough's article. What is striking is that, compared to say, *Pride and Prejudice* or *Persuasion*, the dialogue does not conform to Anne Elliot's definition: 'My idea of good company, Mr Elliot, is the company of clever, well informed people who have a great deal of conversation'. Again with the exception of Mr Knightley, those who are clever in Highbury are not particularly well-informed. While Austen on several occasions remarks on the importance and, in spite of appearances, the moral penetration, of conversation which enters into domestic concerns (117, but also *Persuasion*, of Mr Elliot), the place which draughty corridors, and letters which may or may not be in husswifes, and the merits of Cromer against Southend occupy in the novel's dialogues means that Emma's satire of Miss Bates as flying off in the middle of a thank-you to the state of her mother's petticoat is halfway credible. The quite exceptional focusing on the small, the banal, the unimportant makes the dialogues at once both objects of parody and parody. Emma is caught by this – she threatens to take up carpet work at 40 or 50, she has not read much (a bad sign in *Pride and Prejudice* or *Persuasion*). Who cannot sympathize with her as, waiting for Harriet at the door of the shop, she gazes at the little Highbury has to offer in the way of distraction? Mr Cole's carriage horses returning from exercise, the post boy, William Cox letting himself into his office are the limits of what she can expect, but what she gets are an old woman returning from shopping, the butcher on his delivery round, children looking at gingerbread in the baker's window and dogs fighting. And yet we do not have another, later, Emma's resentment of this downgrading of expectations, already not very high here, for this Emma is both thematiser of and vehicle for the exploration of such triviality. At the end of the paragraph comes the remark: 'A mind lively and at ease can do with seeing nothing, and can see nothing that does not answer' (233) – and indeed up loom Mrs Weston and Frank Churchill. What in Yonville would have been a stray cat is here a lead back to a theme I shall touch on later, that of 'resources' and to that of the nature of the novel, deliberately framed in terms of a dialogue with 'nothing', with a reality that misses preappointment but does not disappoint – things 'answer'.

The parody of novels is readily apparent in such passages as the commentary on Emma's failure to beseech Mr Knightley to give her up in favour of Harriet, or the famous remark about the language of her acceptance of the offer of marriage: 'What did she say? Just what she ought, of course. A lady always does. She said enough to show there need not be despair – and to invite him to say more himself' (431) – how different from Elizabeth Bennet's provocation and reception of Darcy's second proposal, or indeed from the marvellous cancelled chapter in *Persuasion*, where, though there is a deliberate use of small detail, none of such detail, however funny, is the vehicle of parody.

In *Emma* there is, then, a relentless training of attention on the unimportant, typical of satirical parody. It is in the passages of 'skaz' in the novel that this relentlessness comes home. 'Skaz' in Bahktin's definition is a discourse which is highly individualised, and yet also oriented towards another speech act. It is a kind of 'double-voiced discourse', a narration which has the intersection of two voices and two accents (184). While Austen produces such in her speeches of Miss Bates (often to a second degree, in that Miss Bates quotes others), there is one remarkable incident where she develops 'skaz' in an original way. The commentary on the strawberries (358-9), we gradually understand, is Mrs Elton's. But she is leading the way for the others and the nonsequiturs could certainly be Miss Bates's – the punctuation is definitely the latter's. The commentary is unattributed and reduces to wonderfully garbled telegraphese, or sometimes gardening notes, with only one main verb. The manner of writing here makes of this know-all flow, this stream of platitudes the voice of us all. Emma herself, when talking of her drawings ('no great variety of faces') to Mr Elton, does not do much better, she also produces 'skaz', though she manages main verbs (45). Behind both there is another voice, amused and acerbic, another accent, giving warning of the blabber.

The novel and Emma's imaginings have been read as reflection by Austen on her own resources, her own creations (Gilbert and Gubar). The very qualities of imagination allowed rein in her novels are those which in a character in the novel can cause damage to others and doom her to slightly ridiculous blindness. One might extend the scope of the argument to the satire in the novel. The remark about Miss Bates, that she did not have the intelligence to frighten those who might hate her into respect, has been the subject of penetrating comment (Harding, 1940). Like her, 'neither young, handsome, rich, nor married', Austen has the wit and intelligence to force limits through fear to outward expression of contempt; but satire, while bringing the laughs to one side, is unpopular in society – Miss Bates's popularity is being remarked on (see also Lady Middleton's view of the Dashwood sisters). The paradox of literary satire, explored for instance by Molière or an associate in the *Lettre sur la comédie de 'L'Imposteur'* that we are brought to laugh at in others what yet would obscurely induce fear should we realise it were being criticised in ourselves, is pointed at by the remark on Miss Bates. The resources in satire, which Miss Bates does not have, the 'intellectual superiority to make atonement to herself' (21), are those of the book.

Emma is a novel about little things, and about the resources, or their lack, to deal with them (both Emma and Mrs Elton speak of their resources). Style of address, use of language in this novel on two occasions appear such 'little things'. Of Mr Knightley, and referring to Emma's parody of Miss Bates's logorrhoea, Mrs Weston says, 'little things do not irritate him' (225). Little things, 'minute particulars', according to Mr Knightley in a later moment of self-satire, are only made interesting by 'woman's language'; men deal 'only in the great' (472). Knightley holds himself outside such confines.

Marilyn Butler argues 'the final irony is that this most verbal of novels at last pronounces words themselves to be suspect'. The paradox of the novel is that 'although so much of the action takes place in the inner life, the theme of the novel is scepticism about the qualities that make it up – intuition, imagination, original insight' (273). But *Emma* is also about, and talking about trivia, and in that, it develops the satiric tradition. The language of the novel, and language in the novel, reflect, with an amusement tinged just occasionally with a hard bitterness, the chatter but also the unselfpitying because partly unconscious 'liveliness' and 'ease' by which the trivial is made do with. The dialogism here – if it is here – would not be between embodied cultural or historical instances but between various modes, I might almost say moods, were that not too interior, too indulgent (Butler is right) by which the ordinary may be turned into a novel. Virginia Woolf belongs to this line.

An icon of this right at the end, marvellous in its dead-pan humour, relates speaking of the trivial and fear of death:

> The others had been talking of the child, Mrs Weston giving an account of a little alarm she had been under the evening before, from the infant's appearing not quite well. She believed she had been foolish, but it had alarmed her, and she had been within half a minute of sending for Mr Perry [the apothecary]. Perhaps she ought to be ashamed, but Mr Weston had been almost as uneasy as herself. In ten minutes, however, the child had been perfectly well again. This was her history. . .(479).

Such doing with little things and without the sardonic is possible in the novel largely, though not wholly, through the figure of Knightley. A kind of measure of the stylisation of the whole, he screens us from too great a flavour of satire, providing a benign sense of something slightly remote, something more than the brilliantly modulated comedy and yet banal triviality of the whole set of events that make the novel.

Bibliography

Austen, J. *Emma*. In *The Novels of Jane Austen, the text based on collation of the early editions*. ed. R.W. Chapman, vol. iv of 3rd edition in 5 vols., and vol. ii of that in 2 vols. Clarendon Press: Oxford, 1933.

Bahktin, M. 'Discourse Typology in Prose'. In Matejka and Pomorska, 1972.

Booth, W. *The Rhetoric of Fiction* Chicago: University of Chicago Press, 1961.

Bradbury, M. (1962). Jane Austen's *Emma*. In Lodge, 1991.

Butler, M. *Jane Austen and the War of Ideas*. Oxford: Oxford University Press, 1975, 2nd edn. 1987.

Chapman, R.W. *Jane Austen's Letters*, second edition, Oxford University Press, Oxford, 1952.

de G******, Mme. *Les Sympathies, ou l'art de juger par les traits du visage, des Convenances en Amour et en Amitié* . Paris: Chez Saintin, 1813.

Gilbert, S. and Gubar, S. *The Madwoman in the Attic*. New Haven: Yale University Press, 1979.

Harding, D. W. 'Regulated Hatred: an aspect of the work of Jane Austen'. In *Scrutiny*, VIII: 346-62, 1940.

Hobson, M. *The Object of Art: the theory of 'illusion' in eighteenth-century France*. Cambridge: Cambridge University Press, 1982.

Honan, P. 'Sterne and the Formation of Jane Austen's Talent'. In Grosvenor Myer, V. (ed.). *Laurence Sterne: Riddles and Mysteries*. New York: Vision and Barnes and Noble, 1984.

Hough, G. (1970). 'Narrative and Dialogue in Jane Austen'. In Lodge, 1991.

Kant, I. *Anthropologie*. In *Werke*, vol. 10, Wissenschaftliche Buchgesellschaft, Darmstadt, 1798.

Lodge, D. (ed.). *Jane Austen: Emma.*. rev edn. London: Macmillan, 1991.

MacDonagh, O. *Jane Austen: Real and Imagined Worlds*. New Haven: Yale University Press, 1991.

Matejka, L. and Pomorska, K. (eds.). *Readings in Russian Poetics; Formalist and Structuralist Views*. Cambridge, MA: MIT, 1971.

Page, N. *The Language of Jane Austen*. Oxford: Oxford University Press, 1972.

Pound, E. *Literary Essays*. ed. T.S. Eliot, London: Faber and Faber, 1968.

Trilling, L. (1957). '*Emma* and the Legend of Jane Austen'. In Lodge, 1991.

1. Though the view *is* connected by the narrator with Englishness on two occasions: the Knightley brothers' greeting (*Emma*, 99-100) and Mr Knightley's distinction between French and English amiability, the first merely an effect of a good manner. This self-characterisation could be profitably be compared with Kant's account of the character of different nations (Kant, 1798, part II, C).

2. Remember also the career of her favourite brother, Frank Austen, who became an Admiral by his own efforts, not by adoption into wealth. Knightley is a serious manager of his home farm, a deviator of paths to group his fields (107).

3. Translations of *Pharsamon*, particularly relevant through its theme of the misleading imagination, and *La Vie de Marianne* had been published, the latter in multiple editions.

4. See J. Mander, *First Person Narrative and the French Novel 1730-1740*, forthcoming with the Voltaire Foundation, Oxford.

Men in Early 19th-Century French Women's Writing

Alison Finch

The French Revolution and its immediate aftermath had been a time of optimism, then disappointment, for feminists. The Revolution itself had raised hopes that women might now be given rights equal to men's, only for these hopes to be crushed both by male revolutionaries and by the shortly-following repressive legislation introduced by Napoleon. Thus, in 1791, Olympe de Gouges had published a widely-read *Déclaration des droits de la femme et de la citoyenne* in response to the *Déclaration des droits de l'homme* adopted by the National Assembly in 1789. But Gouges was guillotined in 1793 and the day after the public prosecutor told a delegation of Republican women that she had met a fate suitable for all women who departed from the domestic sphere to which nature destined them. And Napoleon's laws, which relegated women to the status of minors and made divorce illegal, were felt by many to have put women in a worse position than during the Ancien Régime. Intelligent and imaginative French women of the early part of the 19th century were, then, faced with a doubly disturbing issue. First – from whatever standpoint – they were still thinking through the implications of rebellion by lower against upper social orders. Second, they were more aware than ever before that another kind of hierarchy co-existed with the visible one that the Revolution had bloodily tried to overturn: the hierarchy of 'men higher than women'. Many French women writers in the first three decades of the 19th century do interweave the two issues. In their works, 'male' is often identified with 'noble rank' while 'female' is identified with 'low social rank'.

Of course this identification is not the only lens through which men are seen in early 19th-century French women's writing. The more sympathetic male characters are often portrayed as having 'female' traits themselves, for example Germaine de Staël's melancholic Oswald and Claire de Duras's gentle Olivier and Edouard. Fathers can be more supportive of daughters than the mothers are, and indeed are sometimes said to pass on their own desirable characteristics to these daughters (Cottin's 1806 heroine Elisabeth, educated in part by her father, has his 'extraordinaire énergie', 22-3). Brothers and male cousins become especially important in these early 19th-century works – not solely to titillate with the image of incest, as in Chateaubriand's *René* (1802) and others. For they can be supportive of erring sisters or female relatives. And if a brother or male cousin has always been a heroine's soul-mate – as in Cottin's *Amélie Mansfield* (1803) and Duras's *Olivier* – this suggests that boy and girl have grown up together as intellectual and psychological equals and that nothing but the accident of gender differentiates them.

One critic has gone so far as to claim that when gentle or depressive male characters appear in novels by *men* of the period, these male authors are attempting a take-over bid of what was commonly thought of as female sensibility. But the presence of such characters in women's fiction also, and the words and deeds of open-minded fathers and brothers, suggest that both men and women writers of the period are experimenting with a blurring of rigid gender divisions in a spirit of generosity as well as imperialism.

An association between 'maleness' and 'upper-class-ness' is not, then, all-pervasive in these works. When it does appear, we must remember that 'class' as a literary structuring device has antecedents – post-1789 female writers did not, of course, invent it. Numerous European writers had already created situations in which unequal social status, or the attempts of 'lower-class' individuals to leave their station, made sometimes for an uneasy form of tragedy, or more usually for comedy (as in the 17th-century Molière's *Bourgeois Gentilhomme* and *George Dandin*). In 18th-century France, Marivaux's novel *Le Paysan parvenu* (1734-5) portrayed social mobility. Notably, Rousseau's *Nouvelle Héloïse* (1761) had affirmed the value of merit over rank; the noble Julie falls in love with the 'commoner' Saint-Preux, whose qualities of mind and heart should in all reasonableness (it is repeatedly stressed) outweigh the supposed virtues of rank.

In 18th-century England, Richardson's *Pamela* (1740-1), amongst other works, gave a central function to class, however conservative the eventual outcome of the plot.

Nor were early 19th-century women writers the first to make some kind of link between an attachment to rank on the one hand and double standards vis-à-vis women on the other. Pregnancies outside wedlock, and characters of illegitimate birth, had already played a part in raising questions about the validity of 'noble' or 'ignoble' birth – again with literary effects ranging from the entertaining to the tragic. Illegitimacy had shaped the plots of such 18th-century novels as Fielding's *Tom Jones* (1749) and some fiction by the 18th-century women writers Charrière and Riccoboni. Although more subdued in the structure of *La Nouvelle Héloïse* (Julie miscarries her baby by Saint-Preux, who does not even know about it until afterwards), illegitimate pregnancy is nevertheless symbolically crucial in that novel as the physical proof of a love that is 'natural' in all senses. Generally speaking, the depiction of illegitimacy had by definition been interwoven with questions about women's reputation and sexuality on the one hand and questions about rank and arranged marriage on the other.

Finally, Montesquieu's *Lettres persanes* (1721) had already, some hundred years earlier, associated 'oppressed social orders' with 'oppressed women': the rebellion in the harem symbolised other kinds of rebellion.

So when similar associations recur in early 19th-century works by women, we may ask whether their authors are doing any more than turning the barrel-organ handle. The answer clearly is that they *are* doing something more. Even if they were merely repeating situations and 'initiating' discussions already known to be ingredients of successful 18th-century fiction, the mere fact that they have undergone the experience of the 1789

Revolution would differentiate them from their predecessors. This in itself (*pace* Pierre Menard) would make the repetition more than just repetition. These writers have seen the destruction inflicted by the Revolution – often on their own world (Mme de Duras, for example, was an émigrée); however, they continue to suggest that the valuing of rank needs re-thinking. But they do in fact go further than their predecessors. They link social rank with other forms of advantage in an often bold, and occasionally outrageous, manner; their questioning is more direct (sometimes to the detriment of the aesthetic qualities of the works). The status of women is now more clearly than before parallelled with that of other lower-class beings who are denied prestige and privilege; and, implicitly or explicitly, 'maleness' becomes 'aristocracy'.

Thus Mme de Staël at the beginning of the 30-year period, and Mme de Duras towards the end of it, make specific connections between oppressed groups. In Staël's *Delphine* (1802), the heroine, currently being ostracised for a supposed fault against womanly virtue, comments to a friend:

> Elise, we're not like that, we who've suffered: yes, in all relationships throughout our lives, in all countries in the world, *it's with the oppressed that one should live: half of all feelings, half of all ideas, are missing in those who are happy and powerful.*(II 101-2; my italics)

In Duras's novel *Ourika* (1824), the black heroine, adopted by a French marquise, has suddenly realised that she is different: she has overheard a friend of the marquises remarking that this black girl will never find a husband unless it is one who is paid to marry her, for what man would want black children? This throws Ourika into a turmoil of misery and self-loathing; but when the French Revolution comes she has a moment of hope. (The novel is set in a period some 30 years before it was actually written.) She thinks that in this upheaval ('grand désordre') she may be able to find a place in society: 'all forms overturned, all ranks now mingling, all prejudices vanishing' would bring about a state of affairs where she would be less foreign ('moins étrangère') (25). More than blackness is at stake here. The triple repetition of 'all' in this statement widens the picture to one of a general reconsideration of all kinds of fixed classification. Black = saleable or unmarketable woman = lower-class.

As well as such broad statements, there are individualised situations in these novels where different meanings of 'ranking' intermingle. Léonce, the hero of *Delphine*, is not simply queasy about Delphine's views on women; he also reproaches her for being too politically liberal. So powerful is his sense of rank and aristocratic reputation that Delphine opposes his ingrained ideas, not only to social liberalism but even to religious principles and a more general morality; she tells him that he would not so readily believe calumnies against her unconventional activities if he had not made a quasi-religion out of 'the model and the memory of old Spanish customs, military and chivalric ideas. . . you've turned "honour", and an almost superstitious respect for public opinion, into a religion which you'd joyfully immolate yourself to' (I 421-2). Here, then, is one link between men's attachment to aristocratic honour and the adherence to sexist stereotypes. In both this novel and *Corinne*, Staël's critique of arranged marriage spells out more forcibly than most not only its degrading and exploitative character but the fact that it is inseparable from the assumptions of the nobility.

Delphine also includes, amongst 'the oppressed', women *and* men who are additionally disadvantaged. For example, Delphine (or her acquaintances) periodically discuss the undue importance attached to women's looks (e.g. II 17-18, 210-16). The ugly woman either cannot marry or will be married only for her money. Ageing has almost the same results: it means the woman, but not the man, will gradually die to the world; she will no longer be heeded and her only consolation will be her children. But women's ugliness and ageing are not the only physical signs of lowered status. In one episode – marked by a typically Staëlian blend of crassness and insight – Delphine describes a marriage between a woman of her acquaintance and a blind man. The woman had been 'riche, jeune, brillante', but had given up all this to look after her blind husband, in whose misfortune she goes so far as to see benefits: in her words,

> his accident means he has to spend his life in the bosom of his family, it means he depends every moment of the day on my helping hand, on my voice, on my presence; he *was* able to see me in my early youth, so he'll always have the same memory of me, and as for me, I'll be able to carry on loving him with all the charm and enthusiasm of love, and without the shyness that comes from the loss of prettiness affecting the way I express my feelings.
> (I 439-40)

This callousness is preposterous. But for present purposes we can simply extract the point being made, which is that the husband's infirmity places him on the same footing as his wife: not only does he become as dependent on her as women normally are on men, but the loss of her looks as she ages will now not matter. Thus a bodily disadvantage in a man can 'equal' the state of being a woman (not, of course, news for Freudians).

By the time we reach the end of *Delphine*, the cumulative picture strongly implies a communality of interests between political liberalism, the cause of women and the cause of the physically deprived – deprived whether through infirmity or age. An unmistakable liberalism also governs certain characters in the works of the best-selling novelist Sophie Cottin; albeit sporadically, they put forward more egalitarian ideas than might normally be expected in a pot-boiler. Of particular interest is an illegitimate son in her novel *Amélie Mansfield* (1803). This young man, Adolphe, displays an acute sense of his disadvantaged position in society and raises both directly and indirectly a variety of questions about rank, and women's 'misdemeanours', from a different perspective from that of the other characters. For example, he will not collude with the deceptions or class-hatreds of the aristocratic characters, making the point that *because* of his illegitimacy, he must be perceived, and perceive himself, as thoroughly honourable. Indeed, Adolphe often morally 'trumps' the nobles to whom he is related. One of them, a crazed matriarch named Mme de Woldemar, is consumed with hatred for her niece, the Amélie of the title. For Amélie has married beneath her and has thus simultaneously let down the family and departed from everything a woman should be. And now, still worse, she has formed a liaison with Mme de Woldemar's son – a liaison which Mme de Woldemar does all she can to destroy. But in a final climax Adolphe tells Mme de Woldemar that he will reveal her hateful behaviour to society (the 'monde entier'); at this, she deplores the fact that she is thus reduced to the point of an 'obscure man without any name' having the right to reproach her (III 182). Morality, then, visibly triumphs over both snobbery and sexism: Cottin, in this novel and others, is making a simultaneous critique of undue attachment to rank and of the rules governing women's sexual behaviour.

Duras, in all three of her novels, conveys poignantly the sheer acuteness with which the 'disadvantaged' suffer. We have already seen that in *Ourika* the disadvantage is both social and physical. In *Edouard*, the disadvantage is purely social, and now attaches to a man, for the hero is lower-class and the heroine upper-class. Edouard is middle- not working-class, but he might as well be a peasant or proletarian, given the anguished drama he reads into the disparity. In the course of highlighting the 'unnaturalness' of this situation, Duras suggests that it is not simply Edouard's gentleness that makes him 'feminine'. His low social status almost makes of him the woman and his beloved the man. Edouard himself draws attention to the mixing of gender roles and social status in a kind of 'mise en abyme' for the whole novel: 'But is it by a woman that you should be protected and supported? In this artificial world, everything's upside down, or rather it's my passion for her that's changing natural relationships in this way' (77). For him, 'inferior rank' is equivalent to 'woman's status'.

Less obviously radical works of the time explore similar issues. In *Laure d'Estell* (1802), Sophie Gay shows an upper-class family gladly accepting back into the fold a daughter who has run off with a young abbé and become pregnant by him; thus Gay too suggests that illegitimacy should lose its stigma, and that the concomitant prejudices surrounding 'low birth' and 'women's shame' may give way to something more liberal. In her later *Léonie de Montbreuse* (1813), the heroine's eyes are opened to her suitor's irresponsibility, not just by the fact that he flirts with other women of his own class, but – in the key episode – by the fact that he tries to seduce or rape a servant girl (the text is discreet about the degree of force used but there clearly *has* been force). Thus an exploitative attitude to all women, and abuse of the lower class, are neatly combined. This is not a particularly original episode (antecedents exist in, for instance, Beaumarchais's *Le Mariage de Figaro*, 1781); but in other novels of the period, too, men's harsh or exploitative treatment of servants is taken as an indication by heroines that the men are likely to be unkind to them too. Conversely, kindness to those of lower classes is interpreted as some kind of guarantee of decent treatment of women in general.

Finally, even in the often empty rhetoric of *Valérie*, Mme de Krüdener's 1803 version of *René*, there lurk somewhat sharper-edged suggestions that undue attachment to rank is a thing of the past, and that love and sensitivity supersede this. The hero Gustave, himself of noble birth, stresses that real sensibility can have nothing to do with notions of social standing:

But high society – that class whose ambition, grandeur and wealth separate it so markedly

> from the rest of humanity – high society seems to me like an arena bristling with lances, where, at every step, you're frightened of being hurt; mistrust, egotism and self-interest, the born enemies of everything that's great and fine, keep ceaseless watch over the entrance to that arena, and there they lay down laws that stifle the generous, pleasing impulses which raise up your soul, make it better and hence happier (131).

The description of Gustave's death is also significant. It is accompanied by reminders of his mother's early ambitions for him: she wanted him to be capable of bearing arms and being like his noble ancestors; she took him as a baby into the family portrait-gallery and addressed one of the portraits thus: 'Look at my Gustave: he'll try to be like you' (299). But because Gustave dies from the excess of his feeling for Valérie, all these ambitions die with him; his line, it is emphasised, is now extinguished. At one level this is simply a fetid ploy to make readers draw out their hankies. But it does also oppose love to the so-called splendours of a particularly 'masculinized' rank. Even if Krüdener is only pandering to what she perceives as the tastes of her audience, what is interesting is that she feels the need for the pandering to take this form. Her novel is modelled on *René*,

but this particular stress is not in *René*.

Let us end, not with a novel, but with a poem which exemplifies many of the tensions I have been describing. In 1819, the poet Marceline Desbordes-Valmore writes a fable, 'The Glow-worm', in which a swaggering glow-worm presents himself as lord of creation and, more particularly, as superior to 'common-class' worms, the 'plebeians' of the fields:

> All those commoners, those worms who crawl round in the daylight, that plebs of the fields which envies me – I feel sorry for them, they offend me in my huge dwelling-place [i.e. the sky].

They are 'born for a vulgar destiny', whereas he 'is the illumination of his court'. But Philomèle the nightingale sees his glow, and although she has 'sought no prey during the whole day', she eats the glow-worm in order to 'carry on being able to sing about her grief'. Desbordes-Valmore is to some extent being derivative: we are bound to be reminded of La Fontaine's fables about boastful animals being devoured or humiliated by other animals – or proud oaks being destroyed by the wind whereas humble reeds survive. Nevertheless, there is a fresh perspective here too. The French for nightingale, 'rossignol', is masculine, but to give the bird its Greek myth-name Philomela enables Desbordes-Valmore to make it feminine. Thus the glow-worm is not simply punished for his aristocratic pride in an illusory status, he is punished by a female – and one who sings, like the poet herself. There is also doubtless a pun in the reference to 'vers roturiers' ('common-class worms'). *Ver* as a singular noun can mean only *worm* – thus the glow-worm himself is never more than a worm; but *vers* can mean either *worms* or *line/s of poetry*. Desbordes-Valmore herself was one of the rare early 19th-century French writers to be of working-class origin. She wrote, if you like, 'vers roturiers'. The destruction of upper-class (and male) pretensions can, then, become the stuff of the songstress's art: 'she eats him, to carry on being able to sing about her grief'. So this violent and self-reflecting poem both embodies and goes beyond what is implied by the novelists.

These women writers' linking of all kinds of disadvantage was to play its part in a more general 19th-century literary movement, that which revalued and promoted the 'lowly' – in choice of subject, in descriptive writing and in diction. It was also to provide, or strengthen, the foundations for some mid- and late-century political and fictional writing about women. For example, the Saint-Simonians, still more consistently than earlier feminists, identify 'woman' with 'working-class' or even 'slave'. And creative writers increasingly choose not just middle-class women as heroines but women at the very bottom of the social heap (say, Hugo's Cosette in *Les Misérables*, 1862; Zola's Gervaise in *L'Assommoir*, 1877; or Maupassant's prostitute in *Boule de suif*, 1880). When these early 19th-century women authors 'voice men' through images of rank and 'ranking', they are helping to set the stage for succeeding works by both women and men, whether imaginative or discursive or both.

André Gide: the Reader's Seduction[1]

Naomi Segal

This essay sets two semi-fictitious figures in front of each other. One, Gide, is here involuntarily immobilized like any object of criticism or desire, with all his intrinsic subtlety or flexibility ambiguously accredited to the perceiver. The other is myself, undertaking a feminist analysis of this dead white homosexual male from a position which needs explanation and perhaps justification. I shall try to do justice to both the complexities of Gide's position in gender and sexuality and also the ambivalences that make me direct at him a critique more complex than when it was disentangling the desiring motives of Flaubert, Mérimée or Prévost. On what authority and with what aim can an anti-homophobic but heterosexual-identified female critic work on Gide? What is feminism to do with gay men?

André Gide, who died in his eighties in 1951, is perhaps unique among a rich generation of French gay writers. For one thing, unlike both Proust and Wilde, he believed it right to speak of homosexuality in the first person. For another, his apologia for pederasty, based in a Platonic tradition, seems to look both back and forward in its strange combination of good citizenship, natural hedonism and pure masculinity. Gide is the 'straight man' of twenties gay creativity: in more or less overt contrast to his contemporaries Wilde, Proust and Cocteau, he rejected the inversion theory and the varieties of [male] femininity as true perversion (and hence loathsome). At the same time, he lived with and off the [female] feminine in a number of ways: the 'mystical orient' of his life was his cousin Madeleine Rondeaux,[2] to whom he committed himself in early adolescence on learning of her mother's adultery, marrying her 13 years later following the death of his own mother and just a few months after he had euphorically discovered pederastic pleasure as an emancipating identity. He probably had no sexual contact with Madeleine but 28 years after they married he had a child with Elisabeth, the feminist daughter of his friend Mme Théo van Rysselberghe – to his disappointment, it was a girl – and he lived more often in the large apartment in Paris adjoining that of Mme Théo and occupied from time to time by Elisabeth and her child and his one-time lover Marc Allégret than on the family estate in Normandy where Madeleine lived near her own extended family and waited for his visits.

And what of his desire? Gide's parents were bourgeois Huguenots, his mother from a well-to-do business family in Normandy, his father a southern-born academic. His father died when he was 11, and his upbringing was that of an isolated boy surrounded by strictly religious women, his mother in particular, with her large square body, sideways unsmiling eyes and embarrassing dress-sense, representing simultaneously all that is negative in a prescriptive and proscriptive religious education and all that terrorises Western culture as a dominating feminine. Madeleine appears to have been her desirable substitute, the mirror in which he looked for his own reflected face, the fixed point from which he continued to make his limited escapes, the pole by which he measured creative emancipation. With her went the same religion, more tenderly packaged but still feminised as the soul which opposes the body. The wife in the house, the spirit (more mystical than stringent now, or so he tried to make it) possessing the body from within – what does the body do to escape these? It dwells in closed rooms, at first, and learns of pleasure in the form of sin, battling with the tireless 'temptation' of masturbation in a way we can only gawp at nowadays. Later it absorbs itself in friendships, intellectually freer but still chaste – in his late teens and early twenties, when Madeleine was refusing him, Gide describes himself as 'virgin and depraved'[3] – and it finally defines itself in the discovery of real warmth and multiple pleasure in the wordless embrace of a brown-skinned boy in the sand outside Biskra. He is horrified by penetrative sex, seeing in it only violence and predation in the briefly evoked scene of his friend Daniel descending under a black coat vampire-like over the frail body of an Arab boy. Gide comments:

> He laid him on his back, on the edge of the bed, at right angles; and soon I could see nothing but, on either side of the grunting Daniel, two slim legs hanging down. As for me, who can only understand pleasure when it is face to face, reciprocal and without violence, and who often, like Whitman, get satisfaction from the most fleeting [*furtif*] contact, I was horrified both by what Daniel was doing and by seeing Mohammed accept it so obligingly.[4]

As an adult, he publishes a solemn and frustrating journal explicitly aimed at the public, starting from 1939, and a string of fascinatingly direct and indirect fictions; he travels, cruises and roosts; he plays mayor and juror in Normandy and amateur ambassador, sycophant and critic in Africa and the USSR; and he preaches a strange sensual pleasure, that of *attente* (expectancy, waiting) which, with its psychological corollary of *disponibilité* (availability) is poised midway between release and absention.

Put all this together and we find a man who seems to desire two things: a feminine mirror he may both fix and abjure, and a masculinity he seeks in the child, preferably brown or bad or both.[5] He lives in voluminous clothes, in which he 'settles himself' when he reclines to read,[6] and embarrasses his friends in railway stations or cinemas by his roving eye, his gawkiness, his habit of shedding underwear or losing suitcases.[7] His second family call him 'the Bipede' [*sic*, pronounced 'Bypeed']. He argues, with Plato, that desire is to do with stopping short, pleasure is in *waiting*, and that the man-boy bond is not indulgence or exploitation but pedagogic and educative, and yet in his fictions the older man is always the simpler, even stupider, of the two, and the knowing child invites while the man holds back in ignorance. Just once in his writing an adult comes near to seducing a child, with a hand slipped into the shirt-front then creeping further down - and the boy leaps away, tearing his collar, runs down to the end of the garden, dips his handkerchief into the rainwater tank and rubs his face, cheeks, neck and body to get rid of the contaminant touch – but here the grown-up is a woman, the same adulterous aunt whose negative figure guided him to the love of the pure girl-cousin.[8]

This pell-mell of details should suggest what a complex thing we undertake when we look to any life, available only in texts, in order to analyse the other's desire. Nothing is nearer to theory, and further from embodiment, than the simplification of people into this or that identity. But if to apprehend is always to oppose (though not necessarily one to one, and if possible without hierarchy), let me begin by trying to arrange the elements of Gide's life into a number of oppositions for us to think him by.

The first opposition is male/female. Female his main educators and some of his 'best friends', wife and daughter; male his schoolfriends, his fellow writers and copious correspondents, and his lovers – the last two groups seldom overlapped. Then class: Gide's rare contacts with people other than wealthy middle-class intellectuals (Sartre, with fair justification, despised his writing for being only about 'rich kids') were with tenants on his wife's estate and the boys he picked up. Colour coincides with class here, for the latter were very often also non-French, 'Mediterranean' street boys or other children met on his travels. With the opposition masculine/feminine the picture becomes more complicated. It is tempting, and perhaps convenient at least as a preliminary, to set up a chronological argument here. In this scheme, up till 1918, when he fell in love with a young family friend, Marc Allégret, who for the first time offered Madeleine a serious emotional rival, gender seems to have functioned along the lines of a conventional oedipal/Christian split: the female/feminine as a mirror-soul in which perfection can be glimpsed and aimed at, haunted of course by the horror of a sexuality which is its dimly thinkable obverse; and the male/masculine as the body-self which exists against it to rebel or be controlled, the universal 'us' of Goethe's 'the eternal feminine draws us onward'.[9] After the crisis precipitated by Madeleine's recognition of Gide's new love, he begins work on *Les Faux monnayeurs (The Counterfeiters)* (1926), the first fiction in which there is, he claims, no version of her as moral pole, and returns to *Corydon* (1911, 1920, 1924), in which the feminine is what a good pederasty pushes aside, both in male inverts and in the female consort who, as in the Greek idyll, is left free by her masters to enjoy a chaste domesticity; here femininity no longer has, it seems, that mirror-function in which Narcissus gazes and knows not if he desires himself as boy or girl.

Then there are other oppositions. Jonathan Dollimore in his Gide/Wilde dichotomy argues that it is Wilde who overturns the depth theory, using paradox and play to advocate an aesthetic of surfaces, Gide who holds to theories of depth-meaning and high seriousness.[10] Indeed this is true of both the periodically Christian Gide and the writer of *Corydon* whose apologia justifies a sometimes absurd argument in terms of a 'deeper' masculinity of social and natural rightness. But it is not true of the desiring Gide whose fantasy cleaves to the skin, to the pleasures of touch or embrace,[11] and to a relation of pleasure with his own body which remains primary in his encounters with others. It is no chance that he quotes in *Corydon* the dazzling aphorism of Chamfort that love in society is 'the exchange of two fantasies and the contact of two epiderms'.[12] Gide's sexual aesthetic is the sculptor's: surface is not so much the tease of a penetrative gaze – stone drapery suggesting an impossible unveiling – but actually the only level there is, not thickness but a journey of the two-dimensional line around a solid space. Let us oppose the Wilde and Gide principles, then, not as theories of surface and depth but as two positions on the relation between skin and its covering. Just as it is impossible to conceive of Wilde unclothed, even in his imagined nudity, so Gide seems always to be reaching a clothed arm towards skin – and stopping there. Sartre once wrote of the way in which [masculine] 'possession' occurs less by ingestion or penetration than by making a mark on a surface: the line of a skier, the mapped colony, the caress of a breast.[13] This, it seems, not penetration, is Gide's fantasy of possession: neither to 'take' nor be 'be taken' but to be *allowed to touch*.

The body for Gide, then, is male and understood in specific transgression of the Christian *noli me tangere*. To touch one's own flesh – his first fiction, *The Notebooks of André Walter* (1891), bounces with the effort to resist this simple temptation, which the seven-year-old Gide first discovered to be a sin when he was suspended from school for masturbating and eating chocolates at the same time. And from this, another opposition: the flesh as own and other. Is it, when the pious adolescent resists the desire to masturbate, the body as self or as other that is being desired? Gide speaks of transgressive desire personified as the demon, specified as 'l'Autre',[14] and we can, I think, assume that in touching or resisting touching his penis he is dividing his self into two along the castratory lines of a familiar Freudian prohibition. For him, masturbation also implies a more specific and perhaps unusual question. Temptation resisted is temptation repeated. It may often be that what is fantasised and refused is a one-act drama, the arc of a rise which ends in detumescent orgasm. But Gide was multi-orgasmic, as he joyfully affirms in his autobiography.[15] Perhaps, then, we are to understand the pleasure/unpleasure of masturbation as sin to be the fear of unstoppable repetition. He writes of the terror of spending himself to the point of idiocy or insanity - that is the only closure he can conceive for his surrogate André Walter, who dies mad. Fluidity, the flow of release, may in itself be the fear,[16] as we recognise from the imaginary of our folktale heritage, with its stories of sorcerers' apprentices, who cannot halt the discharge of the magic porridge pot without the intervention of the parental Other.

Along with the desire of the skin, then, is the desire/fear of repetitious flow. In Gide's texts, in the place of couples, we often have a different kind of plurality, for the 'innocent' man rarely follows the beckoning boy to consummation; rather, a chain of male others is stoppable only in *Le Voyage d'Urien* (*The Voyage of Urien*, 1893), *Les Nourritures terrestres* (*Fruits of the Earth*, 1897) or *L'Immoraliste* (*The Immoralist*, 1902) by the advent of a female figure who puts an end to the movement of language or desire. In *The Counterfeiters* there is always a younger boy not quite within reach. As in the pederastic tradition, the succession of lovers will continue as long as only beardless youths can be desired, for each child is disqualified for love when he becomes a man; but more children will be born as the lover himself grows old. To turn around Lacan's pessimistic dismissal of heterosexual intercourse, in pederasty, it seems, there is no couple.

If, then, this sexuality looks to another while still always also being turned towards the self, how can we understand those kinds of sameness and difference that are sought at the instant of desire? All the evidence I have offered so far of Gide's modes of desire shows that, in seeking an other he wanted a body that would both endorse and espouse his own, skin to skin, and yet also be that other by which he could position his subjectivity: man to boy, white to black, middle-class traveller to Arab servant, educator to wild child. These are, of course, both images of idealised selves and embodiments of difference; they may be exploitation or temporary surrender. And they may perhaps not be so very different, as processes, from either his desire for the unsexualised female other or from the pleasure and risk involved in solitary masturbation, whether narcissistic or joined to fantasy.

In all these oppositions, I have not yet broached the most obvious one: homosexuality / heterosexuality. Central without being clearcut, it is difficult to situate in Gide's life. He proposes to resolve it by a sharp genderising split between deep, pious and lasting love, unsexual and female-directed, and sexual desire, impermanent, promiscuous and skin-deep, which was directed only towards boys. But as his love for Marc Allégret and his fathering of a child illustrate, ultimately the dichotomy does not hold. This problem raises another issue – in which we can no longer understand desire as wholly connected to sexuality. Gide appears to have needed – and as a powerful person to have been able to have – homosexuality and heterosexuality in equal measure, located in a number of centres and theoretically kept apart, in mutual ignorance, and exemplarily suspended both in his writing and in his speaking life.

For all this, let us not forget, takes place now in language, since it is past and gone and has left only a trace to know it by. Gide's daughter and others hold the unpublished material but the millions of published words are ours to plunder. And now I must come to the real issue here, which is how and by what right I am undertaking this plunder.

One answer, the less conscious, is a motive of sexual voyeurism and I will come to this later. The other is conscious and engages fundamentally with theoretical questions of the relation between a feminist reading, undertaken as a critique of masculinity in culture, and the textual object of a gay male writer.

However overtly confessed, feminist criticism of male-authored writing is an oppositional activity, motivated by anger and acquiring by its own logic a triumphalism wholly different from the euphoria that belongs to what Elaine Showalter once called 'gynocritics' – the rediscovery, identification and explication of female-authored texts. That the political difference is something to do with canonicity is proved by the rather more complicated task that faced the 'gynocritic' of George Eliot or Virginia Woolf; in the latter readings, something of feminism's second-decade discovery of its own divisiveness began early. I am aware that I have stayed with the criticism of men's writing for 20 years or so because of the joys of a now-inverted chase – we the hunters, they the prey, and psychoanalysis the undisprovable method for highlighting the murkier areas of their 'unthought'. Their fear, envy and bitterness against women, unpleasant enough to read, can be endlessly pleasurable to expose.

It is important to recognise, I think, that this unilateral attack, justified still by millenia of prejudice and oppression, remains pleasurable even when the feminist critic understands that she is among the relatively privileged of her sex, is perhaps being paid (by men and others) to carry it out in conditions of fair comfort, and that not only is there no such simple thing as 'us' and 'them', but there never was. I still want to muscle in on/grub inside/tease the secrets out of male writing; it is what I do, and it is a Zuyder Zee which is far from cleared. But the conditions are irrevocably changed. Feminists can no longer claim an innocent triumphalism. We know too much about our own complicities and the complexities of any position on any spectrum of power.

With Gide, I want to argue, I face a very complicated knot of differences. He was wealthy, leisured, white and culturally assured from childhood. When he travelled, published or seduced, it was as a powerful man. Nowhere in his writings does one discover a voice unsure of its right to be heard; he is, in other words, always masculine. His masculinity operates in relations with a variety of others – women, black people, children, working-class people, readers, animals, posterity – whom he holds in a position of distance, coloured sometimes by respect, sometimes by desire, sometimes by a rarely admitted contempt (his shameless antisemitism is an exception). This mastery is a fascinating mixture of pedagogy and coquetry; he is the ideal target for a feminist critic, who seeks an address not meant for her and disinters exactly how it is not meant for her. But in other ways he is vulnerable in the way that women are – in certain ways as a hysteric, as a Protestant, as someone whose body, voice and appearance drew embarrassed attention in public places – but much more than this, as a homosexual.

There is no doubt that Gide put his reputation on the line by certain more or less overtly confessional texts – far more directly than Wilde, Cocteau or Proust, however much these others may have been voluntarily or involuntarily outed. Any heterosexual critic retains a privileged position in relation to that, woman or not, which demands due recognition and respect. But what interests me most about Gide are the ways in which his power-position (his *masculinity*) functions within the writing of his homosexuality. Unusually, he writes as a gay man dealing overtly with femininity as his other, whether it resides in women, men or himself and whether he commands/contains it in action or in fiction. If all first terms of a binary parasitise the second, if masculinity is that thing which lives off and out of femininity (again, understanding the latter as immanent anywhere) and if it is the job of feminism to continue asking after the place of the feminine – then how does this gay man live off and out of the feminine in the texts we read him by?

With his usual charm, Leo Bersani has recently confessed that many gay men do not much like women, in a 'more or less secret sympathy with heterosexual male misogyny'.[17] Of course this is true, in a way inevitably more complicated than the (already labyrinthine) way in which heterosexual men dislike women. The man who valorises the phallus in himself and his love-object has the woman as potential rival and, with a feminist heterosexual woman, will also have her as critic, dedicated to the devalorisation of what he prizes. The word 'femininity' occurs no more than once in *Homos* (on p. 111) but is implied and exploited everywhere. For where some gay men get off on the 'suicidal ecstasy of taking their sex like a woman' (p. 19), they are living a fantasised femininity which has no more exact relation to the female body than to their own – less, indeed, since those conventional aspects of womanhood which are less sexually suicidal, like the wish for endorsement at the price of pastoralisation, are roundly condemned. Femininity for Bersani, then, is a privileged signifier as long as it occurs in men, that is, in gay men, and only in certain gay men, at certain moments. It has to do with positionality conceived literally rather than politically. The woman's position, taken by a man, confers a familiarly masculine pride.

Gide does something different but no less absolute. He too robs women of their fire in the name of a deviant masculinity. But to say this is to highlight only one side of the interest he offers feminism. The feminine exists in his texts differently both from the traditional between-men operation of heterosexual homosocial writing and from the other kind of exclusion/exploitation that we find, say, in Bersani or Genet. He relies on women's feminine as a measure of something else which is not women's and not feminine but he does it in the name of a different (surface) sexuality and a different kind of relationality (familial but not oedipal).

Feminism has grown up rather conventionally since it sprang out full-grown aged about 20 in 1970. Quarrels with father and (differently, of course) with mother have given way to other explorations of generational relations. We theorised (late) maternity and now we are theorising the menopause. Of course we also talked siblings and other differences, but essentially (*pace* Deleuze and Guattari), Oedipus held pretty solid and the relation between generations was still comprehensible on a model of the domestic incest motive. None of this has gone; it still remains to be dissected. But with the advent of lesbian, gay and queer studies, the differences have become different. Who inherits now?

I would like to suggest that lesbian/gay/queer studies offers the feminist critique a possible model of relationality which is neither vertical nor genealogical and a conception of the communicativeness of desire – love, pedagogy or pollution – that has nothing to do with inheritance. Such models do not exactly abandon the profit motive of the reproductive family but they turn it aslant. They are unlikely to do without triangularity but perhaps they are abandoning the shortest distance between the three points. Generations without generation: this is what the homosexual model can offer a feminist analysis of power.

Gide evades the oedipal pattern by taking a sideways step away from the parent/child plot to that of uncle/nephew. There is a history for this: it is no coincidence that bastardy so often hid its shame under a supposed uncle-nephew relation, nor that Gide took the family romance theme of bastardy from Romanticism, updating Julien Sorel's quest for a new *nom du père* into the much sexier Lafcadio and his entourage of educating uncles.[18] The masculine chain that I mentioned earlier is different from the genealogical one: not so much by circular or triangular links but by the mini-war of the chess-board, it crosses generations in a knight's move. Being seduced by your much older cousin (effectively an uncle, and with the permission of your mother, who sees in him a loving educator with no taint of exogamy) is safe sex, pedagogic, not incestuous. Plato would have approved. While Romanticism initially explained incest as the only true innocence – in *Paul et Virginie* (1788) and *Atala* (1801) Bernardin de Saint-Pierre and Chateaubriand designed colonial Edens where everyone had access to 'those ineffable unions, when sister was bride to brother, love and fraternal friendship mingled in the same heart and the purity of the one increased the delights of the other'[19] – Gide brings back chastity to desire by a different family relation. But only on one side of the gender variable. The seducing aunt is a horror and a danger – for the same reason that colonists of sexuality always take more care to control women's transgressions: because we are vessels. The image of dirt in the scene from *La Porte étroite* here connects in perhaps an unexpected way with the horror of Daniel's vampiric 'possession' of Mohammed. Both introduce into a forbidden space something pollutant called femininity.

The French term for a 'queen' is *tante* (aunt). Gide's repulsion from the seductive aunt in both senses is a fear of the feminine in desire which makes it something other than chaste, socially justified and skin-deep. Penetration is not safe. To be so it requires either an extra skin of rubber or a monogamy so certain that it is almost familial – and here we smile knowingly at the poverty of the trust any of us might still naïvely attribute to the family relation. In a world so permeable that we no longer define crime/ work/sex, etc. as that which happens outside the four walls of domesticity, where is the safe space? Love and cleanliness? Manliness? Is that what Gide is telling us?

Telling us? In *Les Nourritures terrestres*, the narrator addresses a named narratee, Nathanaël, in a familiar blend of tease, instruction, arousal and evasion, framed at start and finish by the exhortation to 'throw this book away, leave me, go out and live/let me live instead'.[20] If not the desired boy, then whom? Refusing the aunt's seduction, Gide clearly did not intend to seduce any nieces.[21]

And here I want to place the sexual motive of the feminist reading. There is a seductive tease in not being addressed by a writer's desire, especially if that desire is the only point of the text where need escapes from prideful decorum – I shall return to this later. Where Gide lets himself momentarily look a fool – as who does not when addressing the beloved – we can catch him satirically, and knowing ourselves outside the circuit of that appeal, be as ruthless as we like without the usual risk of offence to the vanity of men. But, vulnerable for his moment, is he then still the enemy? I have not yet decided this. Gide's unself-conscious lust, lust of the skin for his pastoral Amyntas, both affirms and breaks him as a man. Does he ever lose face? He looks like 'a criminal or a madman',[22] but is neither outlawed nor abashed. He never drops his guard because he never quite needs to. If, as I suggested earlier, the thing he is not letting himself lose is still his masculinity, then perhaps this can only be understood in terms of his final inability to desire.

Gide was a notorious flirt. The term most commonly used by his friends is *coquetterie*. Pierre Herbart judges that all his actions were motivated by a wish neither to be disappointed nor to disappoint. The flirtation is not even mainly sexual: the 'furtive satisfaction' of his desire seems to have demanded less ceremony. He wanted, like many a star, to be loved severally but exclusively by all those whom his solipsism could magnetise.[23] But how authors operate with their acquaintances may not affect the fact that their books are instruments of seduction. The question is, when I read, how do I attend to that siren call voiced for or against me? Barthes wrote in 1973: 'the text is a fetish-object, *and this fetish desires me'*.[24] Peter Brooks, fourteen years later, exhorts us to 'refuse a text's demand in order to listen to its desire'.[25] The delight of one man and the suspicion of the other are both claims that the text, popping up out of its author's body's motive, smells me out with or without the aid of pheromones.

A feminist critic treads unwarily into the world of textual desire which, like sex, is rarely meant to go direct from gender to gender. Most published books are, of course, an intercourse between men. I would argue, however, that the man-man play of texts is only homosocial up to a point – it masks a *corps-à-corps* that climbs over Oedipus to murder the mother before, during and after the main course. They are not only passing the port. The reader who enjoys what was not written for her is a voyeur. When I deliberately overhear the tongue of Genet at work on his masculines and feminines, I am intervening on a kiss forbidden to a woman. Gide has better manners but he is also asking me to keep my lips closed when he speaks.

What is seduction anyway? What Strachey called by this term (Freud's original '*Verführung*' means very much the same thing) we may nowadays be more inclined to call rape or abuse. But each of those words is perhaps equally inappropriate for what may be a slow or sudden event involving a complex process of mixed coercion and consent. Whatever the detail, the term implies on the one side an element of resistance deemed appropriate and on the other an overcoming of that resistance considered equally appropriate – though in both cases the arbiter of appropriateness is the seducer alone. The latter blandishes, persuades, tickles or caresses; the seducee lets her- or himself be blandished, and eventually there is no going back or forward. The process can only be carried out across a power differential, with resistance initially narrowing the space and capitulation fixing it either open or closed. One keeps cool, the other succumbs. You may let yourself be seduced, but can you let yourself seduce? We are back with Gide's pederastic pedagogue, who seduces but pleads that he has been led, that the brown-skinned child or laughing boy-scout was the one with the wiles and he, top-heavy with education, more taught-against than teaching.

In the pederastic model of Gide's writing, the only place available, it seems, for the feminist critic is that of the niece whom it radically excludes. But we are unlikely to sit comfortably there. Everything in his turned-about homosexuality has suggested how masculine authority remains intact in the role of author/uncle/pedagogue. Something in our non-negotiated contract makes me just as assertive. Intervening in a story in which I am not wanted, I am positioned as the niece but enter as the aunt. And this perhaps is the last theoretical point to emerge from this *corps-à-corps* between absentees. Consciously, I will not allow my critique to be between generations – neither he nor I is willing to play the child.

But unconsciously? I still have something in my hand. What role in this scenario belongs to the book as 'desiring object'? Like an artfully placed item in a window display, it is to create and control my desire that it appears to solicit me. It invites me to break in, shoplift or incur debt – and all the while I will know that it wasn't for me after all (does it even fit?) because it comes as a message without any sender and whose receiver can only be arbitrary. If this is so, then is my seduction as unintended critic of Gide, which I practise without him, a copy of his seduction of himself in those exhausting nights of resistance of his own flesh? He in his room, with chastity, heterosexuality and the Bible as his defence, and I in mine, determined to catch him at it without exposing myself?

1. A longer version of this article appears in *Coming Out of Feminism?* eds. Mandy Merck, Naomi Segal and Elizabeth Wright, Blackwell, Oxford, 1997. Translations throughout are mine. Publication dates given for Gide's works are for the original French texts.
2. The cited phrase actually comes from Jean Delay, *La Jeunesse d'André Gide* vol. I (Gallimard, Paris, 1956), p. 301; he purports to be quoting a sentence from Gide's autobiography *Si le grain ne meurt*, (*If It Die*) in *Journal 1939-1949; Souvenirs* (Gallimard, Paris, 1954), where, however, it appears on p. 434 as 'nouvel orient' [new orient].
3. In his *Journal 1889-1939* (Gallimard, Paris, 1951) p. 33, March 1893.
4. *Si le grain*, op. cit., pp. 595-6. The contrast Gide is drawing here is not entirely clear, since Daniel is obviously penetrating Mohammed from the front; the phrase 'face to face' (*face à face*) is, I think, meant to be understood literally: what he is expressing is a horror of the exclusive use of the lower body.
5. See *Si le grain*, op. cit., p. 567: 'how beautiful he was! half naked under his rags, black and slim as a demon, his mouth open, his gaze wild'; or pp. 593-4: 'how then can I name my joy at clasping in my naked arms that perfect little wild, ardent, lustful, shadowy [*ténébreux*] body?', (ellipses Gide's).
6. See Mme Théo van Rysselberghe's invaluable *Les Cahiers de la petite dame*, 4 vols. (Gallimard, Paris, 1973-5), for instance vol. 1 pp. 194 or 217.
7. See again the *Cahiers de la petite dame* or, for a briefer and even less starry-eyed view of Gide in his body, the beautifully observed Roger Martin du Gard, *Notes sur André Gide 1913-1951* (Gallimard, Paris, 1951).
8. An early scene in *La Porte étroite*, (*Strait is the Gate*) in André Gide, *Romans; Récits et soties; Œuvres lyriques*, eds. M. Nadeau, Y. Davet and J.-J. Thierry (Gallimard, Paris, 1958), p. 500.
9. Johann Wolfgang von Goethe, the final words of *Faust II*.
10. Jonathan Dollimore, *Sexual Dissidence*, Clarendon Press, Oxford, 1991, pp. 74-6.
11. See *Si le grain*, op. cit., p. 565: 'what attracts me is the trace of sun on brown skins'.
12. Chamfort, *Maximes et pensées* (Paul Attinger, Neuchâtel, [1796], 1946), p. 89.
13. Jean-Paul Sartre, *L'Etre et le néant* (*Being and Nothingness*), Gallimard, Paris, 1943, pp. 672-3.
14. This term has Lacanian resonances now, but in everyday French (normally without a capital letter) it would simply mean '*him*'.
15. *Si le grain*, op. cit., p. 594.
16. And of course the desire; see Delay, op. cit., pp. 200-4, 231, 250, 536-9.
17. *Homos*, Cambridge and London, Harvard University Press, 1995, p. 64.
18. I refer here to the heroes of Stendhal's *Le Rouge et le noir* (*Scarlet and Black*, 1830) and Gide's own *Les Caves du Vatican* (*The Vatican Cellars*, 1914).
19. François-René, vicomte de Chateaubriand, *Atala, René, Les Aventures du dernier Abencérage*, ed. F. Letessier (Garnier, Paris, 1962), p. 131.
20. This paraphrases a set of playful/painful parting gestures in *Romans*, op. cit. (1958), pp. 153 and 248.
21. This is not to ignore the potential and *disponibilité* of a series of young women in Gide: Alissa, Gertrude, Sarah, Laura, Geneviève, even Alissa's mother in retrospect. His fiction is not without its audacious girls, but they are quickly netted by pregnancy or its threat, almost inescapably becoming mothers – and adulterous ones at that – as soon as they are out of the nest. They then produce the bastard who may enjoy in their place, and their lovers will become his uncles.
22. This is the comment he reports Madeleine as having made, with 'more sadness than reproach' when, during their sojourn in Algeria, he spent a railway journey catching at the bare arms of the schoolboys in the adjoining carriage; in *Et nunc manet in te*, in *Journal 1939-1949; Souvenirs*, p. 436.
23. Pierre Herbart, *A la recherche d'André Gide* (Gallimard, Paris, 1952), pp.14*ff*. But Herbart also describes the

suddenness with which he would drop one person when 'the little fever of seduction' (p. 65) passed on to the next one. Enid Starkie – in *André Gide* (Bowes and Bowes, Cambridge, 1953), p. 8 – likens the turned-off tap of Gide's charm to the smile of the Cheshire cat.

24. Roland Barthes, *Le Plaisir du texte* (Seuil, Paris, 1973), p. 45.
25. Peter Brooks, 'The idea of a psychoanalytic literary criticism' in ed. Shlomith Rimmon-Kenan, *Discourse in Psychoanalysis and Literature* (Methuen, London and New York, 1987), p. 12.

Marcel Proust and the Unlovable Narrator

Maya Slater

Did Proust meet Freud? We cannot be sure. He never mentioned psycho-analysis or its creator in print. But his novel reveals a fascination with 'Freudian' topics. He recounts and interprets dreams; he gives case histories of mental patients; and above all, his middle-aged hero-narrator is a neurasthenic ('nerveux'), still smarting from his mother's traumatic rejection of his childish love, who somehow succeeds in undermining all his subsequent sexual relationships and destroying his own happiness.

In his treatment of his narrator, Proust can be said to write from a European point of view: underlying this character portrait is an awareness of psycho-analytic trends current in Europe at the time – an awareness which informs the author's approach and shapes his perceptions. Even if Proust never read the works of Freud himself, he must have known what was in the air. The fact that Proust's Narrator Marcel has been 'adopted' by generations of psycho-analysts, who have written extensively about him, shows that the portrait has a strong affinity with their approach. If Freud had not existed, Marcel would have been a much less fascinating character.

This potentially Freudian slant is particularly evident in Proust's portrait of Marcel's emotional relationships. Proust's thesis, congenial to a psycho-analytical reader, is that Marcel, in his relations with women, is playing out a fantasy, not interacting rationally with his real partner. Proust juxtaposes Marcel's actions and words with those of the current object of his obsession, indicating Marcel's irrationality through curious discrepancies between the two lovers' different interpretations of their situation.

Proust is here venturing into a minefield – writing a first-person account in which he repeatedly has to show the narrator failing to realize the truth, while still making that truth perceptible to the reader. In so doing, as the author of a first-person narrative, he is debarred from resorting to authorial intervention. Proust treads this dangerous ground very delicately. The discrepancy between the narrator's perceptions and the picture presented by the author is slight, almost imperceptible.

Nevertheless, something is awry in Marcel's judgement of Albertine's attitude to their relationship. To start with, we must recall the rather strange premises on which their love affair is based. Albertine is an orphan, of low social standing compared with Marcel, and with an astoundingly relaxed attitude to early 20th-century French bourgeois conventions. She readily agrees to live with Marcel, unchaperoned, in his Paris apartment. Her unconventional lifestyle is given a further twist when Marcel becomes convinced that she is a practising and promiscuous lesbian. More subtly, Proust's portrayal of their relationship is, I believe, complicated by a hint that perhaps Albertine is not as Marcel portrays her – that Albertine the pleasure-seeking, amoral lesbian could be Marcel's invention.

The portrait of Marcel throws us off the scent here: such are his intelligence and clear-sightedness that it seems incredible that he is misreading the whole situation. Indeed, one of the most fascinating, and most poignant, aspects of Marcel's relationship with Albertine is the fact that his obsessional compulsions, which have to be indulged without question, are combined with moments of painful lucidity. These flashes of insight do not seem to help Marcel to control his obsessions. Indeed, so carried away is he by the tide of his own feelings that he may brush aside his own perception, barely acknowledging it. Still, although Marcel himself underrates them, these lucid moments indicate the intelligence and honesty of this character.

But they also serve a second, and very different, function, and one that is almost universally neglected: they reveal a profound discrepancy between the general truths Marcel perceives and the way he conducts a relationship with a particular woman.

Let us look at a significant episode in the relationship between Marcel and Albertine, starting with the moment of insight which accompanies the account, which could be seen as Proust-the-psycho-analyst's interpretation of the behaviour of his character Marcel:

> I was too apt to believe that the moment I was in love I could not be loved, and that self-interest alone could attach a woman to me. (p. 508)[1]

This is the narrator's own verdict on his love affair with Albertine. He is telling us categorically that Marcel saw himself as unlovable in his relationships. Marcel cannot deny that women readily enter into love affairs with him, but attributes this to his wealth. This view further implies that the women are degraded creatures, ready to simulate affection in return for financial reward. In this insightful moment, Marcel shows that he is aware that his response is inappropriate - the words 'too apt' tell us as much. His behaviour in the episode in question fits his formula perfectly. From the moment that he decides, on the flimsiest of evidence, that Albertine is definitely a lesbian, we witness him losing touch with reality and leading us down the paths of a fantasy garden. Although we may feel drawn along by him, we are shown that his interpretation palpably does not fit the facts. Let us look at this moment of discovery in the necessary detail.

Marcel and Albertine are in a train. He is not really attending to her – he is planning to leave her for her friend Andrée, having decided that it is Andrée whom he really loves. He plans to start this new relationship on a note of deceit:

> I would give Andrée the illusion that I didn't really love her; thus she would not tire of me. (p. 498)

Meanwhile, on the train, he tells Albertine coldly ('assez sèchement') that he finds their evenings together boring and that he may well back out of the following evening's engagement. He adds that nothing recently has given him much pleasure. Albertine is hurt but takes his remark in good part: 'That's not very flattering to me, but I won't hold it against you, I realize how tense you are' (p. 498). Marcel explains that he would rather spend his time researching Vinteuil's music and adds patronisingly that his 'petite chérie' is unlikely to have heard of this composer.

Now Albertine unwittingly drops her bombshell. She reveals that Mlle Vinteuil, the composer's daughter, is her friend and that Mlle Vinteuil's girlfriend is like a sister to her. Although Albertine does not know it, as a child Marcel had accidentally witnessed a lesbian love-scene between these two women. So he is immediately convinced that Albertine's revelation that she knows them marks her out as a fellow lesbian. Marcel's first thought is that this terrible discovery is sent as a punishment – the figure of Orestes, preserved by the gods in order to avenge a dead father, arises. Marcel feels singled out by fate and now the time has come 'to make me suffer, perhaps to punish me, who knows? for having let my grandmother die' (p. 499) (in fact, she had died of natural causes, despite all his efforts to secure treatment for her). He is suffering 'the fatal and indefinitely prolonged consequences of bad deeds' (p. 500). However, he now goes on to suggest that his punishment is not for letting his grandmother die but for his past moment of voyeurism – the fact that fortuitously he witnessed the lesbian love-scene. In this way feelings of guilt have immediately rushed in to accompany the sense of doom caused by the revelation. But Marcel does not seem clear as to *why* he feels guilty, and the fact that he has produced two unrelated explanations in quick succession suggests that they are rationalisations rather than genuine reasons.

He next realises that he had had an obscure inkling of the truth before Albertine's revelation but without sufficient *'esprit créateur'* ('creativity of mind') to build on the evidence he had. His perverse satisfaction at this *'belle découverte'* ('wonderful discovery') will be discussed shortly.

The train stops and Albertine makes to get off. Marcel now feels that she is part of him, bound to him by the pain she is inflicting. He begs her to come and spend the night in his hotel. She replies that she is exhausted. He implores her: 'You would be doing me an immense favour.' She good-naturedly agrees: 'Then so be it, though I don't understand.' Marcel books a room for Albertine in his hotel, and himself spends the night in mental calculations. He concludes that it would be impossible for a beautiful girl like Albertine to be friends with a lesbian without being seduced; the fact that the two are still close means that she was a willing partner.

Marcel realises that he can look forward to nothing but suffering in future. At dawn, he demands to see Albertine because waiting for what morning will bring – her presence and his suffering – is intolerable. When she arrives, he tells her that he has just broken up with a woman whom he loved and wanted to marry, and is feeling suicidal. There is no warning that he is going to tell this lie but there is an implied explanation of why he has done so: he feels that it is imperative to hide the cause of his distress but has not the strength to hide the fact of it.

Albertine is sincerely upset at his suffering and Marcel asserts that at that instant the idea that she might lose him as a potential rich husband 'didn't even occur to her, so genuinely moved was she' (p. 503). (The formulation of this comment naturally conveys/creates the idea of her cupidity at other times). She offers to stay with him constantly, to console him.

Marcel now points out the irony of his position – the cause of his suffering (Albertine) is its only cure. She is both 'Albertine my ill' and 'Albertine the cure'. He starts looking to the future, making plans to prevent her from going on holiday with her lesbian friend and plotting to keep them apart at all costs. He will take her to Paris. But already at the back of his mind is the thought that 'in Paris, if Albertine had those tastes, she would find plenty of other people with whom to satisfy them' (p. 503), although he dismisses this thought for the present.

Let us review the events narrated here in the light of the understanding they provide of Marcel's cast of mind.

Marcel begins by 'realising' that he is in love with Andrée. He next makes plans to distress his new beloved, Andrée, by claiming to love someone else. He himself is completely convinced of the need for this but his argument (that this is the way to keep Andrée interested) is not self-evident. Indeed, it is difficult to see how a reciprocal love affair could ever develop from such beginnings, dishonourable for the manipulative lover and discouraging for the beloved. Meanwhile, towards his present companion, Albertine, Marcel's attitude is cold and patronising – he has in any case decided to give her up.

When Albertine reveals her lesbian connections, Marcel experiences simultaneously three distinct and even contradictory emotions. Let us take them in the order in which Proust presents them. First, Marcel assumes that this is a disaster sent to punish him, and then he mentions Orestes, a Greek tragic hero singled out by the gods as an instrument of punishment. His initial reaction is thus an uneasy blend of misery and self-aggrandisement. Now Proust adds a third response: the 'almost proud, almost joyous' satisfaction (p. 500) which Marcel experiences at reaching a new peak of awareness about Albertine (the 'wonderful discovery' mentioned above). This response, though unexpected, is not implausible. It has its precedents in great literature, witness Racine's wicked heroine Roxane when she discovers her lover is unfaithful: 'My joy is extreme.' However, Marcel's exultation at realising the dreadful truth is by definition perverse, in that he is responding positively to something he knows will cause him misery from then on.

The next stage for Marcel is a lengthy cogitation on his new discovery. Detective-like (he will later evoke Sherlock Holmes in the context of his dealings with Albertine), he sifts the evidence and derives the inferences. But his deductions are by no means as self-evident as he maintains. On the contrary, it is far-fetched to claim that a woman cannot have a non-sexual friendship with a lesbian.

Marcel, however, feels that his worst fears are confirmed beyond any doubt. His next act is again governed by contradictory instincts. He summons Albertine because his horror of what he will have to suffer through her is so great that he cannot wait for the ordeal to begin.

Why does he now spin a yarn to Albertine about how he loves another woman to the point of suicide? If it is to get her to treat him kindly, then it works, for she responds with warm concern. But comparing this fabrication with the similar tale he was planning to tell Andrée at the beginning of this episode, we can already detect a self-destructive pattern in Marcel's lies. He wants to bind Albertine to him with indestructible bonds. So he tells her he is not available to have a relationship with her. He hopes to make her feel unsure of her hold over him, just as he planned to do with Andrée. In other words, he is demonstrating his conviction, revealed to the reader in the insightful moment I mentioned earlier, that he cannot be lovable to a woman unless he manipulates her into a false position. But in so doing he is talking himself into an impossible position too. If she believes his lies, the woman he desires will assume that he is permanently unavailable to her. Later in the same conversation he will let slip that he is very rich and plans to give the woman he marries (not Albertine!) all sorts of luxuries (a car, a yacht). This is a crude attempt to make himself seem alluring, based on the assumption, which we have already noted, that Albertine is on the look-out for a wealthy husband. Nothing in her behaviour so far has justified this assumption.

Overall, Marcel has here shown himself unfriendly, inconsiderate, inconsistent and impulsive. But in addition to these unpleasant characteristics, there is a much more touching side to this man, who seems unable to cope with honesty in a relationship, assuming that if he does not lie he will be discarded, and assuming also that his beloved will never tell him the truth. He envisages vistas of pain stretching forward into the future. His pitiable state of mind is so powerfully portrayed that there seems little room for additional insight.

But there remains a crucial question to be asked – does he or does he not seem unlovable *to Albertine*? In reading Proust's first-person account, it is easy to feel so bound up with the introspections of Marcel that one overlooks Albertine, the other partner in the relationship. It would seem appropriate to do just what Marcel never does and look no less carefully at how matters must have appeared to her.

Albertine is returning from an evening out with Marcel, a young man whom she greatly admires ('everyone would like to live by your side, look at how everyone seeks you out', she will say to him next morning (p. 506)). He seems cool and abstracted (thinking private thoughts about Andrée, though she does not know this). He is rude to her, telling her that his summer, spent with her, has been dull. She remonstrates but puts the most polite gloss possible on his behaviour. He is contemptuous about her ignorance of musical matters, provoking her into revealing that she knows Mlle Vinteuil and her friend. She does not make this confession as though it were something to be ashamed of. Indeed, she reminds him that she has mentioned the friend before, though not by name: 'I've told you about a friend who is older than me, and who has been like a mother, like a sister to me' (p. 499). Either she is brazen or this is an innocent friendship. (Much later, she will reveal to him that if anything she exaggerated the friendship, stung by his contemptuous assessment of her musical ignorance, eager to prove that she too had musical connections).

On hearing this terrible news, Marcel's internal mood changes radically – but Albertine does not realise this. Outwardly, he continues to seem dissatisfied and preoccupied, as before. She says later: 'during the whole trip I could sense how tense and sad you were'. She is puzzled when, having seemed perfectly happy to let her get out at her station, he suddenly pleads with her to stay. She agrees to do so 'as a favour' – but it is not an emotional favour but *un service* he is asking of her, help with something, but what he does not specify.

Proust omits details of the rest of the evening – what excuse Marcel gives for wanting Albertine to come with him, what they say to each other. When we see Albertine again, it is dawn. He sends the night porter to ask her if he can come to her room. Instead she comes to his – which adds a farcical note to the proceedings, since his room is next to his mother's and the pair have to talk in whispers to avoid waking her up. Albertine arrives in her dressing-gown, presumably worried that something drastic has occurred to make him summon her at such an unearthly hour, to find Marcel in tears and clearly having spent a sleepless night.

Now it is Marcel's turn to drop a bombshell. He announces out of the blue that he loves another woman and has been on the point of marrying her. This is a humiliating blow for Albertine: Marcel has treated her as his girlfriend all summer, embracing her passionately during night-time carriage rides, taking her to meet his friends, and never breathing a word about a rival. But when she sees him weeping over another woman, as she believes (and Marcel himself tells us that she does indeed believe him), her response is spontaneously kind and considerate: 'My poor little one, if I'd known I'd have spent the night by your side' (p. 503). Marcel tells us for a fact that her normal response would be to regret losing such a rich suitor. But her words contain no evidence of such an unspoken thought. She sincerely urges him to consider marriage: 'but you should marry the lady. . . my little one, you'd be happy, and she would surely be happy too' (p. 507). Albertine's use of the word 'lady' (*dame*) is revealing. She talks as though she thought of herself as an inferior, certainly in age and probably in rank as well. The words suggest that she does not aspire to Marcel herself but regards herself as beneath him.

As the conversation progresses, Albertine expresses her great admiration for Marcel. She then voices a reproof of his imaginary fiancée for having made him suffer and concludes with naive outspokenness: 'Ah! If I'd been in her shoes. . .' She seems to be speaking from the heart, and clearly does not share Marcel's belief that to attract someone you care for you have to pretend to be indifferent. And the absurd thing is that on one level Marcel does not notice what is staring him in the face: that Albertine's outspoken devotion to him does not make him desire her any less. In other words, Albertine's behaviour and Marcel's own response to it are an illustration of the fact that the principles according to which Marcel is trying to manipulate her are misconceived.

I say 'on one level' advisedly, because Marcel the Narrator, looking back on his behaviour at the time of writing, is able to see through his own past actions. This is the moment when the quotation with which I started this analysis occurs: 'I was too apt to believe that the moment I was in love I could not be loved, and that self-interest alone could attach a woman to me.' He adds that he underrates his own attractions and concludes with ominous words: 'from this possibly mistaken judgement there doubtless arose many of the misfortunes which later befell us' (p.

508). That lucid moment is definitely retrospective, since the Narrator at the point of writing knows what 'misfortunes' are in store.

Marcel the protagonist, however, shows no signs of this lucidity. He does not seem to register the import of the actual words spoken by Albertine. Instead, he continues both to manipulate her and to assume that all her actions and words are those of a selfish pleasure-seeker, who is playing along with him because of what he has to offer, but without giving up her secret double life. Thus immediately after his lucid observation, he puts his own paranoid interpretation on actions of Albertine which, seen from an impartial point of view, would seem entirely innocent, as follows:

Albertine tells him she wants to pay a brief visit to her home that morning: her aunt may be worrying about her absence the night before; she wants to see if she has any mail. She will come back after lunch. Marcel's interpretation is that 'her devotion was already flagging' (p. 508). Marcel insists that she should send someone from the hotel, and stay with him instead. This is how he describes her response to this suggestion: 'wanting to seem kind but annoyed at being taken over, she wrinkled her brow, then, very sweetly, said at once: "That's fine"' (p. 509). Marcel has made some assumptions here – that her genuine response is annoyance at being thwarted, that her amiability is deliberate, not spontaneous. As a result, the reader is encouraged to give her scant credit for her immediate, willing compliance, and to assume instead that she had some secret reason for wanting to leave the hotel.

Marcel's own assumption that it is not through genuine feeling but through self-interest that Albertine chooses to promote their relationship hardens when she comes to live with him in his Paris apartment. Combined with his conviction that she is a promiscuous lesbian, it governs his behaviour towards her during the whole of their life together. Her every action, even her most fleeting facial expressions, half-formed gestures, half-spoken murmurs, all conspire to confirm his worst fears. Marcel is as vigilant and all-seeing as an Argus; but each fresh piece of evidence simply adds to his pain. This blend of suffering and sharp-eyed observation is compelling for the reader. Marcel is bound up in his agony, and he carries us along with him. For us, as for him, Albertine comes to seem more like an instrument of torture than an independent woman with her own reactions and needs. Hence the temptation to concentrate on the relationship from Marcel's point of view. Marcel's reactions, his neuroses, his jealousy, his misery, are utterly absorbing: there seems no need to look at the situation from any other angle than the one he etches for us in such vivid and anguished detail.

But if we assume that Marcel's account of his life in Paris with Albertine gives the true picture, we are again failing to take into account Albertine's perspective. To put it baldly, her lifestyle is quite simply intolerable. She is not allowed to make a noise while Marcel is asleep. She is not permitted to meet any of his visitors: she has to go quietly to her room and wait until they have left. She is allowed to leave the apartment, but only under supervision. She goes out in the afternoon with her girlfriend, the ubiquitous Andrée. When they return, she must go to her room and wait, alone, while Marcel debriefs Andrée about the outing – whether she met any strange women, made advances or arranged clandestine meetings. Naturally she is bound to find out about these interrogations, since she and Andrée are good friends.

In conversation, Albertine has to be very careful what she says. If she mentions a woman, Marcel will probably ask her whether this woman is lesbian. She soon learns to pre-empt the question by volunteering the information herself that she is not. She must never look at another woman because Marcel would immediately assume that she is planning an assignation. But if she complies with his orders, Marcel is highly suspicious of her lack of interest in other girls, assuming that it must be hiding a rampant sexuality.

In his lucid moments Marcel describes his obsessive jealousy as an illness. But this does not stop him from dominating and bullying Albertine with what he calls his 'anxious need to tyrannize' (p. 598). One of his principal weapons is dishonesty. He never tells her the truth but always 'the opposite of the truth' (p. 849-50) – never admits that he cares for her. He consistently pretends that he does not love her, ostensibly to keep her on tenterhooks about the relationship. He pretends to know her secrets to draw truths out of her. He likes to keep her guessing too about his intentions – so changes his mind at the last minute to thwart her projects. What he never does is to compare his behaviour towards her with hers to him. Never does he realize that lying is perfectly compatible with passion – witness the fact that he is passionate about her, yet lies to her constantly. The discrepancy between what he expects of her and of himself, presented to us without comment by the author, makes Marcel seem arrogant – there is one rule for his behaviour but another, much harsher one for hers – and contributes to the impression of him as an unattractive individual.

But the worst aspect of his behaviour is its underlying hostility. Although he professes to be in love with her, he is constantly antagonistic and intermittently longs to be free of her. He sums up his treatment of her with the words 'I was becoming spiteful' (p. 849). At times, he hates Albertine so heartily that he longs for her to hate him back. Significantly, he talks about how lovers in his position want to 'make ourselves loathed'.

Marcel's actions and interpretations are calculated to confirm that Albertine is a sexually insatiable lesbian who pretends fondness for him out of pure self-interest. It does not matter that there is no definite external evidence to corroborate his theory. Her docility and obedience to his whims (which he endlessly exploits) are themselves seen as a devious expression of her dishonourable character. We must marvel at the ingenuity with which any action or failure to act, any statement or any silence, are inexorably interpreted as proof that she does not love him. Marcel constructs a bullet-proof defence against the possibility that he might be an object of love.

As for Albertine, the author provides us with much evidence to suggest that she is genuinely fond of Marcel, until her affection is exhausted and ultimately killed by his treatment of her. We are not, of course, granted any direct insight into her feelings and thoughts but because this is a first-person account we must assume that we are shown exactly what Marcel sees and nothing more: and yet nothing that we witness confirms his hostile interpretation of her.[2]

We have seen that in the context of his relationship with Albertine, Proust's Narrator portrays himself in a profoundly unlovable light. I said at the beginning, however that this side of him is not brought out, but has to be searched for. Looking at the overall portrait of this relationship, we can see that Proust brings off a considerable feat: he manages to convey the impression of intense and moving suffering on Marcel's part; he succeeds in portraying events through Marcel's eyes, so that the reader neglects to take into account how the relationship must appear through Albertine's; and yet, as we have seen here, he allows the perceptive reader to see a different version of events, in which this anguished, suffering hero, who has all our sympathies, is fundamentally misguided, his misery self-inflicted, because he does not believe that he can ever be loved.

Notes

1. Quotations are from Marcel Proust, in Tadié, J.Y. et al (eds.) *A la recherche du temps perdu, III*. Paris: Pléiade (1988). The translations are mine.
2. Marcel himself never feels certain of the exact nature of Albertine's sexuality since all the corroborative evidence is open to doubt.

Further Reading

Bowie, Malcolm. *Freud, Proust and Lacan: Theory as Fiction* Cambridge: Cambridge University Press, 1987.
Halberstadt-Freud, H.C. *Freud, Proust, Perversion and Love*. Amsterdam & Berwyn: Swets & Zitlinger, 1991.
Julia Kristeva, *Proust and the Sense of Time*, translated by Stephen Bann, London, Routledge, 1993.
McCall, Ian. 'Swann dans les bras de Morphee: a Freudian influence on Proust?' in *Neophilologus* 78, 1994, pp. 529-36.
Miller, Milton. *Nostalgia. A Psychoanalytic Study of Marcel Proust*. London: Gollancz, 1957.
Splitter, Randolph. *Proust's 'Recherche'. A Psychoanalytic Interpretation*. London: Routledge and Kegan Paul, 1981.

Man, Proud Man? Women's Views of Men Between the Wars

Elizabeth Maslen

In 1932, *Man, Proud Man* was published in London, a witty collection of commissioned essays by eight well-known women authors writing in Britain.[1] Each essay deals with a specific aspect of man's behaviour within the patriarchal framework of contemporary European society and the tone is teasing rather than polemical: man's pretensions as master, pleasure-seeker, helpmate and collector are mischievously exposed, his attitudes to personal relations, moral law and religion dissected with precise and cheerful malice. The tone is universally civilised, resulting in an overall picture of man, with his taken-for-granted illusion of superiority, as inoffensive and easily read by these indulgently hawk-eyed women. Inevitably, given the titles of both book and essays, 'man' is dealt with in general terms; indeed, in the non-fictional writing of women throughout the interwar years, men are usually referred to collectively. Generalisation, whether in serious feminist debate or, as in *Man, Proud Man*, in largely light-hearted observation, is a useful tool for exposing the inequities within a male-dominated society. Furthermore, in these essays 'man' is a term used in both essentialist and constructivist contexts; as yet there is no readily available vocabulary for separating traits associated with sex from those relating to gender. The problems this confusion engenders in the interwar years are considerable, since there is inevitable blurring of the boundaries between biological and acquired characteristics. Then again, the uniformly witty tone of this collection of essays, a tone which Virginia Woolf had perfected, pre-eminently in *A Room of One's Own*,[2] masks the fact that while these writers may appear to limit themselves to a largely anglocentric experience, many of them, in their work as a whole, reveal experiences throughout the interwar years which show them to be keenly aware of Europe. Europe complicates their depictions of men by confronting them with the legacy of World War One and the burgeoning fascist movement.

So it is intriguing and instructive to read essays in this collection alongside works which their writers produced elsewhere. For one thing, while the requirements of the essay invite and indeed encourage generalisation, works of fiction or of personal reminiscence more frequently feature the individual, thus problematising observations on 'man' as a collective concept. For another, certain legacies of World War One undermine traditional views of masculinity, so that what can be read as a startlingly conservative conclusion in an essay may be read differently when set against other works by the same author. Take the American Mary Borden's essay, for instance, on 'Man the Master: an Illusion': here, she takes up the idea of man the androgyne which

Virginia Woolf explores in *A Room of One's Own* and argues that the creature of traditional masculinity, the Samson,

> the strong man, the man whom any normal woman would recognise instantly as her master and welcome gladly as her lord, simply cannot and does not exist for a woman, save as an illusion and a dream. For he does not and cannot survive intimacy. (p. 25)

He can, in fact, only come to understand a woman

> because he is like her, the subtle and sensitive, effeminate man, the man, in fact, who is not really more than half a man, the other half of him being a woman, quite scientifically speaking, made up of female biological elements. (p. 25)

While this line of thinking is in tune with debates of the time, since Freud's views on basic bisexuality had been familiar for some years, Borden's vocabulary makes her argument ambivalent. Who is this 'normal woman' who wants a strong man, given that Borden does not specify wherein his strength lies? Does his becoming 'not really more than half a man' imply sexual inadequacy or, as in Woolf's essay, a biological trait affecting gender construction?

Borden faces the same difficulty that Winifred Holtby identifies in her book *Virginia Woolf*, also published in 1932 (and where she tentatively suggests 'gender' as a useful term for things other than procreative sex).[3] Holtby observes:

> We cannot recognise infallibly what characteristics beyond those which are purely physical are 'male' and 'female'. Custom and prejudice, history and tradition have designed the fashion plates; we hardly know yet what remains beneath them of the human being. (p. 183)

By comparison, Borden's argument appears simplistic, partly because of semantic ambivalence, partly because of the humorous tone dictated by the collection. For a moment she contemplates a female-led Utopia but undercuts her argument by a conclusion which does not radically challenge the traditional assumption that women are ethereal, their natural partners brawny cavemen: woman, she asserts,

> will find it wise, as her activities multiply, to cultivate increasingly the semblance of frail femininity that the male likes so much.

Possibly – who knows? – if she does this, if she achieves some such division of labour, taking over all tiresome brainwork for herself and leaving him the manual labours only, she may make a new man of him, who will resemble as a twin brother the ideal primitive man who is now nothing save an illusion. (p. 38)

No mention, note, of the club and dragging off by the hair. Of course, this is hardly to be taken seriously, but Borden risks a lot by seemingly endorsing the so-called 'primitive man' as the 'real man', without definition. Even jesting words can keep a myth alive.[4]

Many of the essays in *Man, Proud Man* share Borden's ambivalence: man's pretensions to patriarchal rights are wittily demolished, but there is a sense too of a need to keep the concept of a 'real man' which gives both writer and reader trouble, given the constant blurring of sex and gender.[5] However, in many cases, as I have suggested, these traces of conservatism are illuminated when we explore other work by the authors. For instance, there is Borden's book *The Forbidden Zone* (1929), a series of sketches, poems and stories based on her nursing experiences in the French field hospital she endowed and worked in for much of World War One.[6] The pellucid exposure of the horrors lying in wait for physically mutilated men, as their traditional masculine identity is stripped from them, reveals mutilations not only of their perceptions of themselves but of the writer's perceptions of them and in consequence of her own identity. War has already deconstructed one illusion of warfare for these *poilus*: 'You can read in their heavy jowls, in their stupefied, patient, hopeless eyes, how boring it is to be a hero' ('Belgium', p. 2). Even on the march from the front, unwounded as yet, 'they do not look quite like men' ('The Regiment', p. 23), and in successive sketches, humanity itself recedes: a wounded man and a woman seen on a beach typify helplessness: they are 'no bigger than flies on the sand' ('The Beach', p. 49); a dying man's cries are 'like the mew of a wounded cat' ('Moonlight', p. 51); while later the mutilated 'mew like kittens' (p. 61) and the narrator muses, 'There are no men here so why should I be a woman? How could I be a woman and not die of it?' (p. 60). She traces the loss of her own identity as men lose theirs, and she personifies companions stronger than either: 'a lascivious monster, a sick bad-tempered animal, and an angel; Pain, Life and Death' (p. 54), while she sees 'Pain as a harlot in the pay of War, and she amuses herself with the wreckage of men' (p. 62). Later, at the Somme, inanimate images appear:

> It is arranged that men should be broken and that they should be mended. You send your
> socks to the laundry, and you sew up the tears and clip the ravelled edges again and again
> just as many times as they will stand it. And then you throw them away. ('Conspiracy', p. 117)

And the narrator begins to see the hospital's role as a negative one: 'We conspire against his right to die', she says (p. 119), and 'his body does not belong to him' (p. 121). A poem written at this time pleads to 'the One who drowned the children of Men;/ Let the waters cover the earth again, Let there be an end to it – an end' ('Where is Jehovah?', p. 86). So the light-hearted ending of Borden's essay in *Man, Proud Man* can carry resonances from her earlier work; since she has witnessed mutilations of masculine identity on a scale which shattered her sense of self, one can read the hope for a Samson in a feminist Utopia as a reaction against what war can do to a man, a reaction that could well blind her to other implications which might be read into her portrayal of a 'real man'.

Susan Ertz's essay, 'Man as Pleasure Seeker' certainly benefits not only from comparison with another of her works but from recent research . Her essay appears at first reading to be wilfully outrageous; having established the links between public games and religion in Greece and Rome, she goes on to observe that the 'Englishman's feeling for cricket is close to reverence' and that 'when a man can forget himself he is usually happy. Hence the fact that wars are not yet outlawed' (p. 79). Yet the jump between games and war is apt for the times, as Joanna Bourke demonstrates in *Dismembering the Male*. She shows how, after World War One, women teachers were frequently accused by male teachers of 'feminising the male body', and she quotes from a 1923 issue of *New Schoolmaster* which brags:

> When men wavered, the sports-masters came to the fore, the real men, those who had done big things in the war. . .Where sports-masters lead, the victory is assured. Sports-masters are the real live men, men who know boy-nature, men who mix with men of other walks of life. They are the men who count. (p. 193)[7]

Such stupefying claims are still being made throughout the Thirties, so what in Ertz's essay may read as ludicrous caricature now was not so ludicrous then, even if Ertz, like Borden, softens her attack in her conclusion where she asserts that

> [man] seeks but one thing – the happiness that comes from forgetfulness of self, whether it come through work, drink, women, music, sport, or love.
> And that, I thought, is why men have made, and, I suspect, always will make, the best martyrs, poets, saints, scientists, and clowns. (p. 101)[8]

Again like Borden's, Ertz's final thrust is ambivalent, her mockery coming perilously close to supporting rather than undermining men's traditional right to certain roles. But in the utopian novel she brought out in 1935, under the growing threat of fascism in Europe, there is no such ambivalence.[9] In *Woman Alive*, a future world is pictured in which biological warfare has destroyed all women but one, and she, Stella, at first refuses any part in keeping the race going because of man's obsession with violence. She sees her world (in the 1980s) as evidence of 'men's mess' (p. 81), sees man as merely 'a fighting animal' (p. 99) and grieves for her lonely status: 'a world without women is no world at all' (p. 128). Yet she also blames women as accessories to men's crimes: 'We always wanted to please men. That was our undoing. If men went to war, we played up to them'
(p. 129) and she goes on to claim that 'if you're romantic, you like the idea of war and killing. Why, heaven knows. . . But it's true that romance and killing have always gone hand in hand' (p. 130). It is not until Ertz introduces Alan, the embodiment of a New Man (American, incidentally, like Ertz herself), that Stella agrees to procreation. Not that Ertz sees Alan's role as easy. He has, after all, personally to set the standard for men who are to maintain their sexual identity while radically altering their gender identity; he has to achieve, without a role model, a leap into what Badinter calls the 'reconciled man':

> Neither a spineless 'soft man' nor a tough one incapable of expressing his feelings, he is. . . able to combine reliability and sensitivity, one who has found his father and rediscovered his mother – that is, one who has become a man without wounding the maternal-feminine. (p. 161)

Ertz then pins her hopes in her novel on an altered male consciousness, while her essay suggests that man will always remain the same. This less sanguine conclusion is echoed a shade more grimly by the Yorkshire writer Storm Jameson in her essay 'Man the Helpmate'. She sees man as unalterable, while the need for woman to change her role is ever more pressing, since woman are, after all, 'incorrigible realists' whose values 'can all be estimated in terms of material existence. There is a sense in which all women are Frenchmen' (p. 118) – Jameson is clearly indulging her lifelong francophilia here! But she goes on to develop her sense of woman's frustrated abilities more seriously, echoing Ertz's Stella in a ringing indictment of 'men's mess':

> How to keep silent, with itching fingers, while men bungle the tasks she can do – knows she can do – supremely well? To continue to suffer chaos in Europe, traffic blocks in the West End, meals provided by English railway companies, the procedures of Parliaments, dirty milk, clothes bought to satisfy the odd and insanitary requirements of the headmasters of public schools, slums, the 'pruning-hook of war'? (p. 130)[10]

And yet Jameson's conclusion also suffers a lapse into apparent conservatism, since, while she claims that 'we have been excessively mistaken in what it [the adjective 'manly'] expresses', she does not redefine it, telling us instead that 'every true man rouses in us feelings of respect, admiration, and astonished delight' (p. 135).

But in her novels of the interwar years, Jameson shows her perception of why traditional definitions of the term 'manly' could cause problems. Of all the contributors to *Man, Proud Man*, Jameson has the most clear-eyed view of what the masculinities of World War One have done and are doing to Europe.[11] As early as 1922, in her novel *The Clash* , she writes:

> The Peace Conference sat in Paris. Liberty, with a bloody pate, stalked famished on the ice-bound Neva. Grand Dukes and generals ran about two hemispheres crying Murder, Revenge, and moved by the thought of so much suffering, the victors of the war blockaded Russia, so that Murder had to tighten his belt across his hollow stomach... the new world was born, by the fecund will of one terrible old Frenchman and passionate lover of his country. He had faith only in the negation of faith and saw that an eyeless malice broods over the destiny of man. Lusts meaner than his, and greeds poorer, served him. Youth, that was to have swept the world, rotted unseen to manure it, or living, became absorbed in a search for excitement or bread. The old men did as they pleased. (pp. 267-8)[12]

Throughout the Twenties and Thirties, Jameson's novels trace the rise of fascist masculinity from the ashes of World War One, charting the increasing savagery of anti-Semitism in, for instance, *Europe To Let* (a novel based on earlier journals of visits to Germany and Eastern Europe, and published in 1940).[13] Indeed, Jameson's reading of fascist masculinity anticipates later readings summarised by Badinter:

> Men's studies have noted the close relationship between masculinity and the large-scale repression of a part of oneself. A denial of bisexuality is the condition for the establishment of frontiers. . . The extreme case of the man cut in half is that of the male fascist under Hitler. . . Excessive repression [of the feminine] leads to repressed self-hatred projected outside and objectified in the figure of a woman if one is misogynist, in that of a Jew if one is anti-Semite, and even in that of a man if one rejects his manliness. (p. 122)

The novels of Jameson, rough-hewn though they often are, probe the tragedies of such repressive masculinity throughout the Europe of her day, and equally delight in finding individual men (the individuals she extols at the end of her essay) who do not subscribe to this model. She has a clear perception of different cultural models of manliness, and of the devastating effects of victimisation of man by man.

The Jewish writer G.B. Stern in her essay 'Man – without Prejudice (rough notes)', again adheres to the overall tone of the collection while caricaturing the absurdities of essentialist hostilities:

> No such thing as generic Man. No such thing as generic Woman. Therefore, no such thing as difference between them. . . But Man on the subject of Woman, and Woman on the subject of Man, are equally an expression of fundamental antagonism. (p. 179)

Yet Stern acknowledges her susceptibility to ' "that Cranford feeling" – . . . nothing could go wrong as long as he was in the house' (p. 189), while next moment asserting that

> in a patriarchy, the women who marry into the family are assimilated into it from outside, and bring very little change into the moral blood-stream. Obviously, then, the patriarchal man subconsciously seeks a type that will not offer resistance to matter-of-fact assimilation. (p. 190)

And Stern ends by arguing that the Victorian Barrett of Wimpole Street, tired of the responsibilities of this superiority, has evolved into Peter Pan, as 'Escape from the obligation to have to *do* something about life' (p. 215).

Such witty, inconclusive observation again acquires ballast when one turns to one of Stern's novels, *A Deputy Was King* (1926).[14] Set in 1921, 'when the world seemed strangely empty and drained of all men' (p. 1), Toni, the Jewish protagonist, is tired of her role of business-woman and matriarch of a cosmopolitan family. Besides, 'she has learnt that directly she succeeded in losing a man's interest in the work she did, she promptly loosened and lost it for the girl she was' (p. 4). So Toni, despite her philosophy of 'men are no good', takes a Gentile husband fresh from the War, conceals her business acumen and her pan-European family, and throws herself into the role of 'little woman'. But Toni's image of Giles's masculinity is as illusory as his of her dependent femininity - and besides, 'Giles has the Great War in his system' (p. 311): gassed then, he succumbs eight years later to tuberculosis and to the redefinition of his manly role, both for himself and for Toni, as a result. In this novel, too, traditional Jewishness problematises generalised definitions: we learn of the old Matriarch's 'virile, autocratic epistles' (p. 126), for instance. And quietly we come to realise the scope of difference: while Giles's military experience shapes all his later actions, Richard, his Jewish friend, who has become, to all intents and purposes, an English landed gentleman and renounced much of his heritage, was 'too young until 1917, and then I was interned. I'd been born in Germany, you see' (p. 200). Stern's novels demonstrate what Badinter reminds us of, and which the collection *Man, Proud Man* disguises with its witty unanimity: 'there is no universal masculine model. . . Masculinity varies according to the historical period, but also according to a man's social class, race and age' (pp. 25-6). And, that being so, women may well need to revise their concept of masculinity, as Toni must, so as to accommodate such variations.

Rebecca West, in her essay 'Man and Religion', remains, like her co-contributors, happy to generalise. She asserts, for instance, that 'carnage survived as the most constant phenomenon of the ages because man disguised his motives for making war' (p. 252): simply, he liked fighting and, moreover, 'men have an excess of what the Freudians first identified as the death-wish. . .They liked exchanging the burdensome freedom of the will for the psychologically easy servitude of military discipline' (p. 253). Men are obsessed with their masculine identity, she says; even in religion, 'we see how the masculine temperament, freed from wise control, tends towards repulsive excess' (p. 257). And West ends by asserting, 'it must never be forgotten that while the disciplined feminine mind can attain an unprejudiced view of reality, the masculine mind is purely subjective and sees only what its hopes and appetites dictate, ignoble though that often is' (p. 284).

But while West in later years tended to remain uncompromising in her condemnation of man, her novel *The Return of the Soldier* (1918)[15] is far more compassionate to the individual male: Chris's return to his home with amnesia, the result of shell-shock, disillusions and disgusts his upper-class wife with her fixed notions of masculinity – Kitty 'hates gracelessness and a failure of physical adjustment is the worst indignity she can conceive' (p. 50) – while evoking nothing but tender understanding in his former lower-class lover. Chris, as Badinter argues for similar cases,[16] has regressed to the all-embracing femininity of his early years, whereas Kitty insists that he should and could recover his traditional masculinity 'if he would make an effort', to which her doctor retorts, 'You've been stuffed up when you were young with talk about a thing called self-control – a sort of bar-maid of the soul' (p. 162). Eventually, Chris is indeed 'cured', to Kitty's delight but, as the female narrator sees only too well,

> when we have lifted the yoke of our embraces from his shoulders he would go back to that flooded trench in Flanders under that sky more full of flying death than clouds, to that No Man's Land where bullets fell like rain on the rotting faces of the dead. (p. 187)

The selection of texts explored in this paper illustrates the complex blend of conservatism and radicalism[17] which we find in women's writing between the wars, and goes some way to accounting for it. The legacy of World War One merges into the growing threat of World War Two; for many, the First had shattered traditional views of male superiority, while the urge to rebuild the illusion obsessed those who would embrace fascism. Women writers are on the horns of a dilemma: a dread of the militarism and power complex at the heart of patriarchy, and compassion for individuals who have been robbed of their identity with no acceptable alternative in place. The problems for men are as clear to these writers as they are to later theorists. But their Europe is as far as ours from welcoming unreservedly Badinter's 'reconciled man'.

1. Mabel Ulrich, ed. *Man, Proud Man* . London: Hamish Hamilton, 1932. Contributors: Mary Borden, E.M. Delafield, Susan Ertz, Storm Jameson, Helen Simpson, G.B. Stern, Sylvia Townsend Warner and Rebecca West.
2. Virginia Woolf. *A Room of One's Own.* London: The Hogarth Press, 1929; Penguin, 1963.
3. Winifred Holtby. *Virginia Woolf.* London: Wishart, 1932.
4. A myth subscribed to by Hitler, when he identifies the mass as sharing her femininity, as John Carey reports: '[Hitler explains in *Mein Kampf* that] a woman's inner sensibilities are not under the control of her abstract reasoning, and she feels a vague emotional longing for a strong male to dominate her. So, too, does the mass.' John Carey, *The Intellectuals and the Masses: Pride and Prejudice among the Literary Intelligentsia, 1880-1939* London: Faber and Faber, 1992, p. 203.
5. See Elizabeth Badinter. *XY: on Masculine Identity* 1992 tr. Lydia Davis (New York: Columbia University Press, 1995).
6. Mary Borden, *The Forbidden Zone* . London: William Heinemann, 1929.
7. Joanna Bourke, *Dismembering the Male: Men's Bodies, Britain and the Great War.* London: Reaktion Books, 1996. The article quoted comes from 'Man Consciousness', *New Schoolmaster*, IV. 20 (May 1923), p. 10.
8. For Ertz's comment on 'forgetfulness of self', Peter Schwenger, 'The Masculine Mode' in *Speaking Gender*, ed. Elaine Showalter. New York and London, Routledge, 1989: 'To think about masculinity is to become less masculine oneself. For one of the most powerful archetypes of manhood is the idea that the real man is the one who acts, rather than the one who contemplates. . .To think about himself would be to split and turn inward the confident wholeness which is the badge of masculinity. And to consider his own sexuality at any length would be to admit that his maleness can be questioned, can be revised, and, to a large degree, has been created rather than existing naturally and irresistibly as real virility is supposed to.' (110). I am grateful to Dr Catherine Maxwell for reminding me of this passage.
9. Susan Ertz, *Woman Alive.* London: Hodder and Stoughton, 1935.
10. There is a footnote on the 'pruning fork of war' which reads: 'Sir Arthur Keith in a recent address to the students of a Scots University. The learned gentleman was clearly under some misapprehension of the uses to which sane gardeners put their pruning-hooks. Did he, perhaps, imagine that they pruned away only the best and lustiest shoots? Now, if in the next War, recruits were strictly chosen from men between the ages if fifty-five and eighty-five, Sir Arthur would be able in person to justify his metaphor. Would that not be a profound satisfaction to him?' (130).
11. There were of course many women not represented in this collection who had their own keen perceptions of these things. See, for example, Katharine Burdekin, Murray Constantine, pseud., *Swastika Night.* London: Victor Gollancz, 1937 and 1940.
12. Storm Jameson. *The Clash.* London: William Heinemann, 1922.
13. Storm Jameson. *Europe to Let: The Memoirs of an Obscure Man.* London: Macmillan, 1940.
14. G.B. Stern. *A Deputy Was King* . (1926) London: Virago, 1988.
15. Rebecca West. *The Return of the Soldier.* London: Nisbet, 1918.
16. See Badinter, chapter two (pp. 43-66).
17. This blend of conservatism and radicalism is discussed by Alison Light in her admirable book. *Forever England: Femininity, Literature and Conservatism Between the Wars* London: Routledge, 1991. I suggest here another reason for why that blend persists, even among writers who are keenly aware of problems posed by traditional constructs of masculinity.

Evelyn Waugh's Suspenders

Ann Pasternak Slater

Evelyn Waugh is a singularly appropriate subject for scrutiny in a volume devoted to issues of gender because he represents the unacceptable face of masculinity in two extreme forms. In his fiction, his persistently unsympathetic portrayal of women has been the object of an extended study. In his life, he is notorious as the archetypal male chauvinist pig. Both are misconceptions. Both are instructive. Together, they demonstrate the errors endemic in cross-projection – the risky, wholesale attribution of attitudes inferred from an author's life to his works and the unjustified identification of authorially-held values in the vagaries of his characters.

Matters are complicated by the fact that Waugh's personality came to acquire the status of a fictional creation. He consciously cultivated a caricature persona epitomised by Cecil Beaton's photograph in which he stands, a portly cigar-brandishing country gent in loud checks, barring access to his estate behind the notice, 'Entrée Interdite aux Promeneurs'. The assumption of such an unsympathetic role was an act of public entertainment and private self-defence, a dual motive captured by the more famous sign to Combe Florey, 'No Admittance on Business'. This reversal of the norm firmly yokes Waugh's beleaguered privacy to his professional frivolity. In life as well as art he is the 20th century's Dickensian Great Entertainer. He explains further in the 'Portrait of the Artist in Middle-age', the dispassionate self-analysis opening *The Ordeal of Gilbert Pinfold* and the only candidly autobiographical self-portrait in his work:

> It was his modesty that needed protection and for this purpose, but without design, he gradually assumed this character of burlesque. He was neither scholar nor regular soldier; the part for which he cast himself was a combination of eccentric don and testy colonel and he acted it strenuously. . . until it came to dominate his whole outward personality. . . He offered the world a front of pomposity mitigated by indiscretion that was as hard, bright and antiquated as a cuirass. (*The Ordeal of Gilbert Pinfold*, p. 9)

Neither Waugh nor his work can be properly understood without grasping this pervasive instinct for half-serious self-caricature. The protective burlesque identified in *Pinfold* dominates both Waugh's public personae and the roles he plays in his own works. All his novels draw directly on his own experiences; in most, if not all, the heroes are consciously comic downgradings of himself. This is why the simple correlation of Waugh with his works is so tempting – and so dangerous, when it fails to allow for the distorting glass of self-ironisation.

The portrait of Pinfold also captures the menacing impersonality of Waugh's vision: 'Shocked by a bad bottle of wine, an impertinent stranger, or a fault in syntax, his mind like a cinema-camera trucked furiously forward to confront the offending object close-up with glaring lens' (*Pinfold*, p. 8). Waugh the man was not the only subject for his dispassionate analysis. A comparable detached callousness often governs his fictional portrayal of women. Accordingly, Jacqueline McDonnell adopts a tone of severe charity in the conclusion to her study:

> One has to feel some pity as well as despair for a man who was so obviously crippled. He sees women as adulteresses, as incompetent mothers, as unintelligent, as disfigured by make-up, as ruining stately homes, and in many other unflattering lights. He cannot accept any kind of frailty. Even women being ill nauseate him. (*Waugh on Women*, p. 214)

But some women are adulteresses, many are disfigured by make-up. There is no reason why they should not be portrayed so. Moreover, there are many motives for Waugh's complex attitudes. He was profoundly hurt by his first wife's desertion and in the novels predating his second marriage a number of heroines reflect this bitterness. Kittenish sexuality masking a moral void characterises both Nina Blount in *Vile Bodies* and Brenda Last in *A Handful of Dust*. In *Black Mischief* Prudence Courteney's infantile, pouting promiscuity qualifies her for exclusive retribution as the *bonne bouche* of a cannibal feast – she lives and dies by the flesh. *Scoop's* Kätchen is a more appealingly vapid variant. And yet these women are not merely the expression of a wilful personal animus. There is an outraged personal morality motivating these unquestionably negative portraits; they are a crucial part of Waugh's total moral vision. Inevitably, for some modern readers assuming the virtues of free love, Waugh is bound to appear prejudiced. But - and this is the final, all-embracing point – Waugh is not a misogynist monolith. Many of these women's lovers – Ginger, Basil, Beaver – are equally or more reviled. His satire is directed at both women and men. His positives are as often feminine as masculine. No hero of his approaches the moral status of Cordelia in *Brideshead Revisited,* or Margaret in *Pinfold,* or Helena, the eponymous heroine of his least known, favourite novel. One has to feel pity as well as despair for criticism reduced to such crass accountancy. What really counts is the unique role each character plays in the intricate structure of Waugh's meticulously crafted works. And there is no more fascinating text for this purpose than the unfinished novel, *Work Suspended,* the author's affectionately nicknamed *Suspenders*.

Work Suspended is particularly compelling in the present context because it figures three women, all highly individualised and each belying McDonnell's negative impressions – the supposed heroine, Lucy Simmonds, whose tenderly described pregnancy dominates the work's second half; her young cousin Julia, whom I suspect to have been the intended ultimate heroine; and a universally overlooked minor character of central thematic importance, a Berber prostitute. All three are sympathetically presented, in contrast to Roger, Lucy's cad of a husband, and the difficult priggish hero, John Plant. The novel is also absorbing because it is incomplete: it had to be abandoned with the declaration of war late in 1939 and marks a watershed in Waugh's technique.

In it he first tries out the ample, ruminative style later adopted in *Brideshead* and the *Sword of Honour* trilogy. The shift in mode was only temporarily aborted with the novel's abandonment, Waugh's original, tersely cinematic satiric manner being fleetingly resumed in *Put Out More Flags* and later *The Loved One*. *Work Suspended* therefore quivers at the fulcrum of Waugh's climacteric, and indeed proclaims the fact through the words of its hero, who has reached the same point in his own writing career. Like *The Ordeal of Gilbert Pinfold*, the novel centres on a comically critical self portrait. Above all, it is an enigma yearning for a solution, not only because it was left unfinished but because it survives in two sparely but significantly altered versions which span the war, epitomising Waugh's hopes before it began and his deep sense of desolation at its end.

Work Suspended was started in the summer of 1939, a glowing time for Waugh. His second marriage, to Laura Herbert, had taken place two years before, ending a long period of bachelor rootlessness, uncertainty and unhappiness. After months of pleasurable house-hunting, the wedding-gift of Laura's grandmother enabled them to buy an elegant Georgian mansion exactly answering Waugh's dreams. Their first child was a year old, the second expected in the autumn. While Europe braced itself for war, Waugh himself resolutely turned his back on politics, restoring his house, improving the estate, combing the countryside for cheap Victoriana. His twin passions for Augustan provincial architecture and Victorian eccentricity came to saturate his literary aesthetic. In *Suspenders* they appear in two forms: the new orotundity of style modelled on Augustan prose and the personal eccentricity of the hero's father whose death dominates the first half of the novel. Plant senior is a Victorian artist surviving with absurd flamboyance well beyond his time, a caped figure muttering objurgations at the flats rising round his home, his vast canvases Victorian treasure-houses of detail. Through him Waugh declares his radically reactionary manifesto. His new style is to be a thing of the past, a throwback to the 18th and 19th centuries, in keeping with his new persona, the landed gent of Beaton's photograph. The credo of a defiant dodo.

Work Suspended is a first run at the portrait of the artist later perfected in *Pinfold*. The imperceptibly gradual emotional growth of the pointedly named hero, John Plant, is delicately registered in his progressive relationships with the novel's three women. The novel opens with him wintering in Fez, his latest book two-thirds complete:

> I had been there for six weeks, doing little else but write, and my book, *Murder at Mountrichard Castle,* was within twenty-thousand words of its end. In three weeks I should pack it up for the typist; perhaps sooner, for I had nearly passed that heavy middle period where less conscientious writers introduce their second corpse. I was thirty-four years of age at the time, and a serious writer. I had always been a one-corpse man.
>
> *(Work Suspended, p. 107)*

Plant's situation is modelled on Waugh's, wintering in Fez in 1935 to complete *A Handful of Dust* (a three-corpse book). There is something supremely ridiculous in

Waugh's obviously alter-ego first person narrator being a mere crime writer with fatuous pretensions:

> I took pains with my work and I found it excellent. Each of my seven books sold better than its predecessor. Moreover, the sale was in their first three months, at seven and sixpence. I did not have to relabel the library edition for the bookstalls. People bought my books and kept them – not in the spare bedrooms but in the library, all seven of them together on a shelf.
>
> (p. 107)

In 1949 Chapman and Hall brought out a uniform library edition of Waugh's fiction, with *Work Suspended and Other Short Stories Written Before the Second World War* as its eighth and final volume.

There is no gainsaying Waugh's carefully sustained mirroring of himself in Plant. The difference lies in their divergent personalities. Plant has none of Waugh's exuberant, affectionate vitality. In Fez, Plant, like Waugh, provides for the needs of the flesh by congress with a local Berber prostitute. But the tone in which each describes the same experience is significant. Waugh writes to his friends:

> I go most evenings & take my coffee in a brothel where I have formed an attachment to a young lady called Fatima . . . She is brown in colour and her face is tattooed all over with blue patterns v pretty . . .
>
> (*Letters*, p. 84)

Plant, conversely, forms an attachment to the place, not the person: the blue-light district rather than the blue-tattooed Berber ('The Moulay Abdullah was an orderly place . . . I had formed an attachment for this sole place of its kind which endowed its trade with something approaching glamour'). Plant's Fatima is identical to Waugh's, 'a chubby little Berber with the scarred cheeks of her people and tattooed ornaments, blue on brown, at her forehead and throat', but Waugh's kindling of affection ('v pretty') is gone. Waugh gives Fatima a milk ring, notes her pride in her gold tooth, and thinks she would have preferred something more precious. Plant keeps his Fatima at bay by telling her he has a wife and six children in England. There is a chilly utilitarian impersonality in his sexual dealings:

> She asked about my business.
> I told her I exported dates.
> The date market was steady, I assured her.
> ... That was the charm of the quarter for me - not its simple pleasures but its privacy and anonymity, the hide-and-seek with one's own personality which redeems vice of its tedium.
>
> (*Work Suspended*, p. 124)

Plant's days are spent in an arid, spinsterish routine – living in a cheap, chilly hotel, appealing in its austerity; writing; dining once a week with the Consul when he takes his weekly bath; visiting Fatima at equally parsimonious weekly intervals. The pattern is barely ruffled by news of his father's death. Since others have dealt with the funeral

Plant sees 'no reason for a change of plan' (a phrase twice repeated, emphasising his loveless poverty of spirit), until he is discomfited by a police raid on the brothel quarter. Twice he is constrained to telephone the Consul for accreditation. This, rather than his father's death, impels him to leave:

> I was finished with Fez; its privacy had been violated. My weekly visit to the Consulate could never be repeated on the same terms. . . We had exposed the bare minimum of ourselves; now a sudden, mutually unwelcome confidence had been forced. (p. 125)

Many readers have found Plant vaguely unsympathetic but the effect is clearly far from accidental.

On his return to England, Plant's extreme solipsism is first breached by his grief for his father's death, an emotion long suppressed but released towards the end of the novel's first section. The second is devoted to the quickening of Plant's *tendresse* for Lucy, newly wed to Plant's old crony, the playwright Roger Simmonds. Plant's devotion grows with her burgeoning pregnancy, which is conveyed with a reverential warmth quite alien to the conventional perception of Waugh:

> Couched as she was, amid quilted bed-jacket and tumbled sheets – one arm bare to the elbow where the wide sleeve fell back and showed the tender places of wrist and forearm, the other lost in the warm depths of the bed. . . (p. 173)

However, this glow of love has a chaste gravity Plant attributes to Lucy's state, 'her grace daily more encumbered by her pregnancy; deprived of sex, as women are, by its fulfilment'. One suspects it is just this that allows Plant to give his feelings root-room; his love is unthreatening because it cannot be fulfilled. Roger, unlike Plant, is not in the least interested in his wife's interesting condition and sees Plant as a useful companion for her in the months when his own marital rights are in abeyance. Throughout the novel Roger is a negative touchstone, a character derided for his lack of artistic integrity and political opportunism (he is a cocktail Communist). It is significant that he, who lacks any authorial approbation, should regard marriage in terms of masculine possession:

> Roger was hobbled and prevented from taking the full stride required of him, by the habit, long settled, of regarding sex relationships in terms of ownership and use. Confronted with the new fact of pregnancy, of joint ownership, his terms failed him. (p. 173)

When Lucy goes into labour it is Plant, rather than Roger, who suffers a husband's anxiety. He rings constantly to find out how she is doing. When he is told there is 'some kind of a lull', that she cannot speak but lies there crying, he is intensely distressed:

> I had been smoking a pipe; my mouth had gone dry, and when I knocked out the smouldering tobacco the smell of it sickened me. I went out. . . as though to the deck of a ship, breathing hard against the nausea. . . (pp. 180-1)

It is unfortunate that at this point the Penguin text should have a misprint furthering the common misconception of Waugh's callousness:

> The thought of the lull, of Lucy not speaking, but lying there in tears waiting for her labour to start again, pierced me as no tale could have done of cumulative pain; but beyond my sense of compassion I was not scared.

Both original texts, of 1942 and 1949, read 'I was now scared'.

That misprint is symptomatic. Waugh's attitude to women is widely misread. McDonnell confidently asserts he 'cannot cope' with feminine frailty in general and motherhood in particular; voicing a common complaint, she says he 'never seemed to be present for the birth of his children'. In the novels the heroes abscond likewise and male discussions of pregnancy show an 'even worse . . . extreme lack of understanding', passing crass remarks on the perils of parturition – mothers going mad and bald, babies being freaks (McDonnell pp. 212-13). One might point out – mildly – that the first criticism is both anachronistic (McDonnell is driven by a post-sixties assumption quite inappropriate to the period) and untrue (only a few weeks later Waugh was at Laura's side for the birth of their son Auberon). More to the point is the fact that all the fictional remarks are made by unsatisfactory characters, Roger above all. It is he, not the emotionally maturing Plant, who betrays a callow insensitivity to the genuine dangers of childbirth, to which Plant responds with such painful intensity.

Once the baby is born, though, there is a sharp and quite unexpected reversal in the novel's last two pages. When Plant visits Lucy the next day he finds her 'slack and smiling' and is sickened by a 'pastrycook's atmosphere' in which she calls everyone, from her nurse to Plant to the stuffiest of visitors, 'sweet'. It would be absurd simply to project Plant's revulsion onto Waugh, who was shortly to spend all his days at Laura's bedside. The reasons for his change of heart have to be sought within the text, not outside it.

Truth is one. There is an unflattering accuracy in Waugh's portrayal of the short-lived intimacy we feel for those helping us through labour and the first days of motherhood. He is equally uncharitable in his characterisation of the huffy superfluous male. Plant's miffed stiffness, with which the novel ends, is not amiable. Once again the origins for the portrait are autobiographical. Many years later, in the last two published letters of his life, Waugh admitted to Lady Mosley that *Work Suspended* was 'to some extent a portrait of me in love with you' in 1929, when she was married to Bryan Guinness and pregnant with their first child, but that the friendship 'petered out' after the baby's birth. 'The explanation,' he says, 'is very discreditable to me.' The limitations of Plant's feelings for Lucy exactly correlate to Waugh's next words:

> Pure jealousy. You (and Bryan) were immensely kind to me at a time when I greatly needed kindness, after my desertion by my first wife. I was infatuated with you. Not of course that I aspired to your bed but I wanted you to myself as especial confidante and comrade. After Jonathan's birth you began to enlarge your circle. . .

(Letters, p. 638)

In the novel Waugh conveys Plant's motivation through a series of discreet parallels. In an attempt to pass the hours of Lucy's labour, Plant visits the Zoo, a favourite haunt of theirs, where he meets by chance the man who ran over and killed his father. Atwater is a disreputable scrounger whose earlier ill-judged attempts at apology Plant has choked off. Now he is glad of company, and when Atwater asks for money, gives it to him. Together they go to the cage of Humboldt's Gibbon, where two women feeding the monkeys are overheard to say 'I don't see the point of animals you can't feed'. Atwater's mood shifts from bonhomie to bitterness:

> 'What's amusing about that black creature there?'
> 'Well, he's very beautiful.'
> 'Beautiful?' Atwater stared into the hostile little face beyond the bars. 'Can't see it myself.' Then rather truculently, 'I suppose you'd say he was more beautiful than me.'
> 'Well, as a matter of fact, since you raise the point. . .'
> 'You think that thing beautiful and feed it and shelter it, while you leave me to starve.'
> This seemed unfair. I had just given Atwater a pound; moreover, it was not I who had fed the ape. I pointed this out.
> 'I see,' said Atwater. 'You're paying me for my entertainment value. You think I'm a kind of monkey.'
> This was uncomfortably near the truth. 'You misunderstand me,' I said.
>
> (p. 187)

When Plant visits Lucy and the baby a similar realisation strikes him: 'She did not want me, I thought; Humboldt's Gibbon and I had done our part.' Lucy, too, had welcomed him merely for his entertainment value. Significantly, Waugh had prepared for this theme with Fatima, the young Berber, who also has a demeaning entertainer's role imposed on her. When Western visitors, particularly women tourists from the big hotels, visit the Moulay Abdullah, the prostitutes are made to line up and shuffle through a native dance – a display detested by all the girls, 'who regarded it as an unseemly proceeding'. When Plant witnesses Fatima performing this charade she is 'genuinely and deeply abashed'. Her distress prepares for Atwater and Plant's parallel dislike of their gibbon-like roles – and, for the many who accuse Waugh of snobbery as well as male chauvinism, that grouping should give pause – particularly since it is a cluster in which Waugh also implicitly places himself. When furnishing Piers Court he had acquired a huge pair of portraits of George III and Queen Charlotte, which he initially found disconcerting but ultimately irresistible, noting in his *Diaries*, 'In the library I sit opposite the portrait of George III and have decided to keep it there permanently . . . I think of putting "scribble, scribble" on a ribbon across the top'. Waugh, too, saw himself as another Gibbon.

Lady Diana Mosley told Jacqueline McDonnell that 'Lucy was a prime bore as far as I can remember' – a negative impression she must have raised in those last letters to Waugh, who in his reply denied it being 'a cruel portrait' of her. Yet Lady Diana is right: there is something singularly insipid about Lucy, who has little to recommend her except good breeding and a certain direct authenticity. In the fragment as it stands, Plant's love for her is the novel's second most important subject, balancing the delineation of his eccentric father in the first half. The arrangement of the work in its revised, post-war form, emphasises this: it is divided into two 'Parts', the two wings of a diptych, titled 'A Death' and 'A Birth'. Yet it is clear from a number of embryonic motifs, as well as the decisively disillusioned ending of the fragment, that Plant's relationship with Lucy was not going to be the full novel's main theme, and that, even as it stands, the fragment enshrines the beginnings of a far more important relationship of whose significance Plant is so far unaware – his friendship with Lucy's young cousin Julia.

Julia is an eighteen-year-old staying with Lucy who is a keen admirer of Plant's works; Lucy gratefully employs him to entertain her. She is engagingly described ('bright, dotty, soft, eager, acquiescent, flattering, impudent'), but one gradually becomes aware of a pointed contrast between the relationships of Plant and Lucy's circle, and Julia's with him. Opening the description of his burgeoning infatuation with Lucy, Plant had meditated on the impossibilities of writing about love:

> To write of someone loved, of oneself loving, above all of oneself being loved – how can these things be done with propriety? How can they be done at all? (p. 151)

In his detective stories, Plant says, he has used it as a motive, written it up as passionate, written it down as modest, 'spoken of it continually as a game of profit and loss'. Among his friends this is the accepted mode: when Roger first courts Lucy and finds she is a serious girl he 'played his game accordingly'; among Plant's friends 'it was only by making our relationship into a kind of competitive parlour game that we kept it alive at all'. Even Plant himself, negotiating into intimacy with Lucy, admits 'I moved for advantage as in a parlour game', while Lucy introduces Plant to Julia 'in a manner which had. . . an element of dumb crambo in it'. It is characteristic of Waugh's technique to lay a long fuse like this when he wants to make a particular point. The fuse reaches its destination with Julia. There is none of this game-playing with her. She is unaffectedly direct in her adulation. Seated beside him at the Simmondses' dinner party, she is transparently delighted ('"My word, this *is* exciting," said Julia, and settled down to enjoy me as though I were a box of chocolates on her knee'). During the dinner she is intelligent in her appreciation of his work. This too is significant. She is the only one to appreciate him as a serious artist, no lower-case gibbon. At the end of the dinner party she tells him, with equal frankness: 'Please, I must tell you. You're a thousand times grander than I ever imagined. It was a game before – now it's serious.' Bang!

Julia's adolescent crush on Plant has all the spontaneous generosity he lacks. She is unguarded, forthright, unafraid to risk herself in a hopelessly unequal relationship. Within the ten days of her stay in London she twice asks Plant to kiss her. The first time he refuses (or, in the revised version, kisses her 'paternally on the cheek'). At their last meeting she commits the mild impropriety of visiting his bachelor flat with a farewell gift of cigars he tries at first to refuse:

> 'Don't you see I shall go back to Aldershot absolutely miserable, the whole time in London quite spoilt, if you won't take them?'
> She had clearly been crying that morning and was near tears again.
> 'Of course I'll take them,' I said. 'I think it's perfectly sweet of you.'

Her face cleared in sudden, infectious joy.

'There. Now we can say good-bye.'

She stood waiting for me, not petitioning this time, but claiming her right. I put my hands on her shoulders and gave her a single, warm kiss on the lips. 'Thank you' she said in a small voice, and hurried out. . . Sweet Julia! I thought. It was a supremely unselfish present; something quite impersonal and unsentimental – no keepsake – something which would be gone, literally in smoke, in six weeks. . . (p. 167)

Before Plant even admits his feelings for Lucy to himself, Julia has understood them, telling him 'you're in love with Lucy, aren't you?. . . I can tell. . . And it's no good. She loves that horrid Roger.' Plant may believe himself to be writing of someone loved, of himself loving, but Waugh is writing above all of Plant's *being loved*.

It is this that opens up the vistas of the unfinished novel in its original form. The revised version of 1949 ends with a Postscript in which Waugh firmly closes down all the beginnings he had initiated. Within days of Lucy's baby being born, 'the air raid sirens sounded the first false alarm of the second world war'. From such a perspective, all the preoccupations of the novel are dismissed as mere atavism:

Beavers bred in captivity, inhabiting a concrete pool, will, if given the timber, fatuously go through all the motions of damming an ancestral stream. So I and my friends busied ourselves with our privacies and intimacies. My father's death, the abandonment of my home, my quickening love of Lucy, my literary innovations, my house in the country – all these had seemed to presage a new life. The new life came, not by my contrivance. (p. 193)

But when the first version was abandoned, all these did seem to presage a new life. For Waugh as for Plant there was a house in the country, literary innovations, a new love in which his futurity was contained. Julia is like Laura when Waugh first fell in love with her, 'only 18 years old, virgin. . . and astute'. But I suspect that even that would only have been part of a greater theme. In the original version of the novel, the first chapter is not called 'A Death', but 'My Father's House'. Ostensibly, it refers to the house of Plant's father which is sold off and demolished after his death. But to a literate reader it implies much more:

Let not your heart be troubled: ye believe in God, believe also in me.

In my Father's house are many mansions. . .

(John 14 1-2)

The implication of the chapter-heading is that the projected plan of *Work Suspended* was to be the spiritual growth of John Plant, from a life of sterility and detachment to emotional engagement and finally religious commitment – a *Bildungsroman* such as was successfully completed only after the war in Waugh's 'M.O.', his Magnum Opus, *The Sacred and Profane Memories of Captain Charles Ryder*, or *Brideshead Revisited*. In both novels, the aborted embryo and the fully-formed child of Waugh's Catholic imagination, sacred love grows from the profane. Or so, at least, we can surmise from *Brideshead*:

'It's frightening,' Julia once said, 'to think how completely you have forgotten Sebastian.'

'He was the forerunner.'

'That's what you said in the storm. I've thought since, perhaps I am only a forerunner too.'

'Perhaps,' I thought, while her words hung in the air between us like a wisp of tobacco . . . smoke – a thought to fade and vanish without trace – 'perhaps all our loves are merely . . . hints and symbols. . .' (p. 288)

Perhaps the cigar smoke released by Julia's gift in *Work Suspended* has drifted across the years to this final location. For in many ways the two novels are about the same thing.

Nathalie Sarraute: 'Neither Man Nor Woman Nor Dog Nor Cat . . .'

Ann Jefferson

'When I write I am neither man nor woman nor dog nor cat'

Nathalie Sarraute[1]

In 1959 Nathalie Sarraute was described in an interview as not the sort of writer one would think of 'photographing in her bath',[2] a comment which makes a brief allusion to her sex only to dismiss the topic from the more unworldly agenda of her writing. This was the heyday of the *nouveau roman,* and the most publicised photograph taken of Nathalie Sarraute in that year was one which depicted her standing outside the Editions de Minuit, flanked by Claude Ollier and Samuel Beckett, and in the company of her fellow New Novelists, Alain Robbe-Grillet, Claude Simon, Claude Mauriac, Robert Pinget and their publisher Jérôme Lindon. To be a woman in this group of men may have been an exception to the rule of men but it was one that went entirely unremarked in those terms.[3] It was not until the late 70s and 80s when the *nouveau roman* was on the wane as a collective phenomenon, and *écriture féminine* was on the ascendant, that anyone thought to pose the question of Nathalie Sarraute as a 'woman writer'. However, Nathalie Sarraute herself has always vehemently repudiated the notion of women's writing: 'It is a serious mistake, especially for women, to talk about women's writing [*écriture féminine*] or men's writing,' she warns. 'There are just writings, period.'[4]

Yet this demand for equal recognition could be seen as characteristic of a particular brand of feminist politics which were bred in the 1930s when the issue was not – as it has come to be since the 1980s – the assertion of female difference, but equal suffrage, a cause in support of which Sarraute herself actively campaigned. (French women were not granted the vote until 1945.) The daughter of a man who believed that women 'had something in their brains which reduced their intelligence',[5] and acutely aware of the differences in the educational ambitions and opportunities for the boys as compared to the girls of her generation,[6] Nathalie Sarraute would seem to have good reason to share the broad assumptions and egalitarian aspirations of Simone de Beauvoir, just eight years her junior. Like Beauvoir, she believes that 'One is not born a woman: one becomes a woman',[7] that femininity is, in other words, a social construct. Like Beauvoir too, she believes that work and its concomitant economic independence represents the road to freedom for women. But most of all, she shares with Beauvoir the view that the invention of womanhood alienates women from their status as human beings. In Beauvoir's words: 'The fact of being a woman poses peculiar problems for a human being [*un être humain*].' For men, by contrast, masculinity and humanity are virtually synonymous:

> The advantage that man enjoys, which makes itself felt from his childhood, is that his vocation as a human being in no way runs counter to his destiny. (p. 643 / II,435)

Beauvoir is chiefly preoccupied with the resulting impossibility for women of reconciling work and erotic fulfilment. And although Sarraute eschews both the social and the sexual as topics of literary concern, her discussion of the perception of gender, particularly in the theatre, makes some very similar points to Beauvoir's. For Sarraute, it is impossible to represent the 'human being' as anything other than male. Women, she says, are incapable of appearing gender-'neutral', of being simply a 'human-being.' This, according to Sarraute, is because

> they are always represented as, represent themselves socially as, wish themselves to be – and that's a large part of it – different from men. They have certain habits, certain ways, a certain voice, certain intonations, most of which, in my view, are put on and are the result of upbringing. It would be unbearable to have this play [her own *Pour un oui ou pour un non*] acted by women, because one wouldn't be seeing human beings, one would just see women quarreling. There exists a certain image of woman, which up until now it's been impossible to eradicate, which will immediately be imposed or projected onto these two human beings.[8]

It is no accident that Sarraute should make these comments about gender in the context of the stage, for both she and Beauvoir share the Existentialist interpretation of theatre as a form of inauthenticity, and of inauthenticity as a form of theatre. The stage in this perspective constitutes an arena for specular modes of being in which people can appear only as inauthentically playing up to the demands and assumptions that are mediated by the gaze of the spectators. Insofar as gender is defined for both these writers as part of these socially consecrated assumptions, gender issues are fatally entangled with theatrically conceived forms of inauthenticity. Both for Sarraute and for Beauvoir, woman are trapped in their gender identity by the fact that they are the object of a gaze: that of men, each other's, and their own as fantasised in the eyes of others. According to Beauvoir, women's failure (as she sees it) in the world of work is due to the narcissism which is an inevitable by-product of their condition: unable to forget their own image in the eyes of others, women are incapable of losing themselves in absorption in their work and are consequently doomed to mediocrity. Moreover – and more importantly for the woman writer - this debilitating self-awareness also undermines the work of women who choose to be artists and writers:

> Thus, of the legion of women who toy with arts and letters, very few persevere; and even those who pass this first obstacle will very often continue to be torn between their narcissism and an inferiority complex. Inability to forget themselves is a defect that will weigh more heavily upon them than upon women in any other career.
> (p. 665 / II,469)

Sarraute's very similar sense of the way that women are trapped in a male gaze stems – in her view – both from the way that the gaze imposes a certain image upon them (as in the case of actresses on the stage), and also from the tendency that she ascribes to some of her female characters to play up to the image that men have of them as women: instances where 'a woman *acts* the role of a woman' (Benmussa, p. 140). (I shall come back to this later.) Where Sarraute differs crucially from Beauvoir, however, is in her conviction that the absorption and forgetting of self which in Beauvoir's view are denied to the woman writer, are, on the contrary, given in the very activity of writing.[9] For Sarraute, to write one has simply to close one's eyes to the possibility of being seen. 'I do not see myself,' she says repeatedly to Simone Benmussa in the course of their published conversations. When she goes on lecture tours, thanks to her inability to conceive of herself as someone seen, Sarraute claims she is able – even on the quasi-stage of the lecturer's podium – to find the freedom that Beauvoir believes still to be unavailable to women:

> I have the impression that where I am there is like an empty seat. I can never imagine that when I leave people, they talk about me. This gives me a great deal of freedom. When I'm lecturing in front of students, I am always very free because I don't exist. Words come out of me and go towards them, and those words will get through because they are bearers of something which seems sincere and true. But as to how the students see me? The idea never crosses my mind. (p. 75)

Writing consititutes an extreme version of this scenario of invisibility and absorption:

> I am so involved in what I am doing that I don't exist. I don't think that it's a woman who is writing. The thing which I'm working on is happening somewhere where the female or the male sex isn't relevant. (pp. 140-1)

Sarraute seems implicitly to be contradicting Beauvoir's pessimism about women's writing by claiming that the activity of writing can and does, of itself, confer upon women the dual condition of invisibility and its consequent gender-neutrality so often denied to her characters – both in each others' eyes, and in the eyes of their readers or audience. The woman writer finds exemption from the 'ineradicable image of woman' which in the real world is inevitably projected onto real women because – it would seem – writing automatically equips the writer with the 'cap which makes one invisible' from fairytales which one of the characters in '*Fools say*' briefly finds himself wearing.[10] Unlike the women who step into the visible arena of the stage and acquiesce to the image of woman projected onto them (by men and women alike), the woman who sits down at her desk to write can simply vanish from sight. And as she disappears from view she begins to acquire the status of 'human being' that is the birthright of men, be they actors, writers or anything else.

However, in Sarraute's novels, where everything is a matter of negotiating gazes, the experience of the characters raises questions about such vanishing tricks. In particular the novels question what, ultimately, would guarantee the invisibility that confers immunity from the image projected by the gaze of the other. '*Fools say*' explores more thoroughly than any other novel of Sarraute the experience of this negotiation, as characters who feel themselves to be 'a universe of their own' 'infinite, and without boundaries', are nevertheless viewed by others precisely as 'characters': 'a character which is imposed upon one or which one imposes oneself'.[11] It is important to understand the logic of this dilemma before trying to establish how – or indeed whether – the writer succeeds in escaping it.

The gaze in Sarraute's fiction is almost always the vehicle for the construction of stereotypes and gendered images are common currency in the repertoire of these stereotypes. '*Fools say*' opens with the highly gendered image of a fairytale grandmother who is constituted primarily as a visual object: 'A thing. . . An object, set there before us, on display, on offer. . .' (p. 16/19), a magnet for the fascinated gaze of her grandchildren: 'we couldn't take our eyes off her sweet faded face' (p. 10/11). Furthermore, gathered around this visual focus, the children are conscious of composing a visual scene themselves, 'a charming family picture' (pp. 12/13-14). It is not just social images (fairytale grandmothers, happy families) that are produced by and for visual appreciation. Social consensus is clinched by gazes: an appeal to visual evidence and an exchange of glances that seals complicity, as the following exchange suggests:

> – That's not so, we aren't poisoned, you're the one, my poor fellow, it's you who have
>   allowed yourself to be permeated by it. . . it's plain to see [*Cela saute aux yeux*].
>   They glance at each other [*Ils se consultent du regard*], they nod in assent. . .
> – I agree with you. . . Yes, so do I. (p. 59/75)

The gaze of the complicitous crowd creates its own evidence which the individual who is its object is powerless to resist. A child is told he has a 'menton en galoche' (a prominent chin) and feels his chin actually growing under the pressure of the gaze of the group who has made the assertion:

> On that head that he's now rigged up in, on that face of his, which is exposed to view, like
> their faces, as everybody looks on, it's advancing, lengthening, a chin to which the word
> 'galosh' has attached itself. (pp. 31/38)

This particular character undergoes the experience of characterisation as helpless victim of the views (in all senses of the word) of others, unable to make himself invisible to the eyes of the world.

There are, however, characters who revel in the look of the other and the results are often strongly marked by gender. A character who is variously described by others as 'a poseur', a would-be genius, lives his (implicitly male) role to the hilt:

> full of his own importance. . . Full. Brimming over with himself. Unable to leave himself.
> Fascinated by the image of himself that he projects. Preoccupied with that more than
> anything else. Caring first for that. That's the be-all and the end-all. (pp. 134/171)

Women are even more prone than men to this form of fascination with their image, and are frequently depicted as being both more susceptible to the gaze of the other and more in need of the consecration that it brings:

> She needs to be seen, to spread herself around. . . and he understands this, she must go out,
> take the air, acquire new strength, be admired, sanctioned. . .[12]

Both male and female (in their varying degrees) in Sarraute's universe are created primarily by the specular gaze of the subject before his mirror or the admiring crowd.

The gaze of the other is, nevertheless, always treacherous in Sarraute, even for those who appear to thrive on it. For most, it is experienced as cruel imposition (like the boy with the 'menton en galoche'), or as a spotlight that brutally exposes the subject to view. The character who feels he is protected by a cloak – or cap – of invisibility is occasionally caught in the beam of the gaze of others in ways that he is powerless to control:

> more often than not he has the reassuring impression of moving among them like the
> fairy-tale figure who wears a cap that makes him invisible.
> And all at once these brutal awakenings. . . What's happened? His protective cap has
> been snatched away. . . There he is, exposed... His eyes widen with alarm. . .
> (pp. 28/34-5)

He is forced to concede a likeness in the photograph of himself that the group confronts him with, until they eventually turn away and he is restored to his previous condition of invisibility, 'as though in place of his body, of his face, there were an empty space which their glances pass through' (pp. 30/37).

The blank which the character in question regards as his natural state has a clear resemblance to the cloak of invisibility which Sarraute lays claim to in her own case and which supposedly protects her writing from the gender-producing gaze of the other. This raises the possibility that the division which, according to Sarraute, separates a woman's writing from her fate in the social exchanges of the real world, may not after all be absolute. And indeed, she is perhaps nowhere more harsh in her treatment of 'the woman who *acts* the role of a woman' than in her depiction of the woman writer Germaine Lemaire in *The Planetarium*. There are two women writers who figure in Sarraute's *oeuvre*, Germaine Lemaire and her own mother in *Childhood*, and both are represented in relation to the visual. Sarraute has also spoken of her writer-mother in interviews where she reports that her mother wrote under a male pseudonym, N. Vikhrovski, a cover which was apparently never broken.[13] But Sarraute's depiction of her mother in *Childhood* reveals a woman who, far from living under a cloak of invisibility, is the centre of a huge amount of visual attention. Like the grandmother in '*Fools say*', she is 'delicious to look at'. Apparently carelessly indifferent to mirrors, she nevertheless successfully magnetises the gaze of others:

> I thought she was often delicious to look at, and it seemed to me that that was how she was
> for many others as well, I could see it in the eyes of passers-by, of tradesmen, of friends,
> and, of course, of Kolya.[14]

The mother's writing is also a visual and very public affair: when writing she did not closet herself away from the public gaze, but could be seen sitting and covering page after page with words which are described in terms of their visual rather than their communicative impact:

> what comes back to me is the impression that, rather than to me, it's to someone else that she's recounting. . . no doubt one of the children's stories that she writes at home on big pages, covered in her large handwriting with its disconnected letters. . . (pp. 12/21)

This is the reverse of the model of communication that Sarraute evokes to describe what happens when she lectures to students: an empty space where she is, and words which are received by their addressees in the audience. Sarraute's mother exercises a powerful charm ('in the literal sense of the word, she charmed me' p. 19/28), where Sarraute seeks to 'establish contact'.[15]

Moreover, there is a certain gendering of the literary genres that Sarraute's mother espouses: '*romans-fleuves*, children's stories and novellas'.[16] Sarraute's own attempt to write like her mother (in the story of the Georgian Princess that she writes as a child) is portrayed in *Childhood* as a dangerous brush with the inauthentic and provides a glimpse of the kind of writing that Sarraute ascribes to her mother. It is one that bears a striking similarity to the kind of writing that Beauvoir claims to be peculiarly characteristic of women. According to Beauvoir, women's desire to please and to be accepted in the world of men condemns them to a fatal caution in literary matters:

> A woman is still astonished and flattered at being admitted to the world of thought, of art – a masculine world. She is on her best behaviour in it; she is afraid to disrupt things, investigate, cause explosions; she feels she should seek pardon for her literary pretensions through her modesty and good taste. She relies on the sure values of conformity; she gives literature precisely that personal tone which is expected of her, reminding us that she is a woman by a few well-chosen affectations and preciosities. All this helps her to excel in the production of best-sellers; but we must not look to her for adventuring along unexplored paths.
>
> (*The Second Sex*, p. 666/II, 471)

As N. Vikhrovski, Sarraute's mother may have been in a position to avoid the obligatory gestures of ingratiation typical – according to Beauvoir – of most women writers, but she nonetheless seeks to guarantee her place in a man's world through her literary conformism, her preference for best-selling genres and her refusal to take risks with experimental forms of writing. In short, despite its male signature, the writing of N. Vikhrovski bears the mark of female gender in its generic orthodoxy and in its author's heavy investment in a visual existence.

Much of this also applies to Germaine Lemaire in *The Planetarium*. Germaine Lemaire's desire to be accepted in the masculine world of 'art and thought' takes the form of a particularly narcissistic demand for recognition. This recognition is invariably solicited from men who are incited to grant her rights of entry into their world in exchange for her self-presentation as a woman. Sarraute's portrayal of Germaine Lemaire is highly critical and shows the fictional woman writer to be shameless in her complicity with the self-contradictory contract whereby a feminine identity is used as the essential bargaining counter in her negotiations for membership of a world that belongs to men. Unlike Natacha's mother, Germaine Lemaire has no male pseudonym to alleviate her femininity, and although she is described as having rather 'rough-hewn features', (pp.144/133), the issue on Alain Guimier's mind when he visits her for the first time is her beauty: 'She's beautiful. "Germaine Lemaire is beautiful", they're right, it's obvious.'[17] Natacha's mother may have had a better claim to this epithet than Germaine Lemaire, but the issue is as central for her in *Childhood* as it seems to be for Germaine Lemaire in *The Planetarium*, except that the mother expresses it in the form of an explicit demand: ' "A child who loves its mother thinks that no one is more beautiful than she" ' (*Childhood*, pp.85/94). Germaine Lemaire's demand is not articulated in so many words but it is just as powerful – as the testimony of those who encounter her reveals. Alain comes away from his first visit with the sense that Germaine Lemaire's reputation – beauty and all – is the effect of the response she exacts from those around her:

> it doesn't just come all by itself, fame, a reputation. . . there's a sort of unsated hunger, a need for adulation. . . you can never give her enough. . . she keeps a check, she takes people's measure, she has to put them in their place at the slightest lapse. . . (pp.109/100)

And a fellow member of the coterie tells Alain:

> 'she knows how much you admire her. . . And that's what matters to her above all else. [. . .] You see, for Maine, people are mirrors. They're foils. In reality she doesn't care a rap about people. . .' (pp.177/163)

This use of people as mirrors and sources of adulation would seem to be a cruder version of the response that Natacha's mother elicited from shopkeepers, passers-by and her devoted husband, in whose eyes Natacha regularly saw the image of her mother produced by their admiration.

But Germaine Lemaire discovers that she cannot exercise complete control over the production of her image in the eyes of others, and in an encounter with Alain's father – a man who is deeply sceptical about his son's literary pretensions – Germaine Lemaire feels herself stripped by the older man's gaze not only of the adulation which she craves, but of the gender which the adoring look of her admirers normally guarantees:

> She had suddenly felt herself exposed, blushing, trembling before this gaze from which there poured over her, covering her, the cold spite, the contempt of a man who has been pampered, showered for years with grace, youth and beauty, the distaste of a fastidious connoisseur for a woman. . . but she didn't look like a woman, she was a shapeless, unnamable something, a frightful monster, hair all dishevelled. . .

She is even inhibited from performing the one gesture that Natacha's mother allowed herself a mirror for, namely to push back a stray lock of hair that had escaped from her chignon:

a few forlorn locks, she was aware of them, hung down the back of her neck, she hadn't
dared lift her hand to push them up under her hat.[18]

The most damning element of Sarraute's critique of Germaine Lemaire's dependency on
the gaze of others is in the disastrous effects it has on her writing. The thought is first
tentatively voiced by Alain to his friend in the Lemaire coterie:

> 'But if she's like that, as you say, so self-centred. . . for a writer isn't it. . .? To put it frankly,
> isn't it a failing which could be rather serious. . . A real shortcoming. . .' (pp. 177/164)

The friend refuses to hear these doubts, but confirmation of Alain's suspicions is brought in
the chapter that follows immediately after this conversation. In it Germaine Lemaire finds
herself burdened with the ambivalent accolade of 'our Madame Tussaud', and finally
confronts the fact that the products of her creative efforts are dead: 'Not a breath of life in it.
It's there that everything is dead. Dead, dead, dead. . .' (pp. 185/170). The female demand
for admiration consecration proves to be incompatible with authentic, living writing.

Sarraute's depiction of women writers in her work would seem, then, to suggest first,
that nothing automatically exempts them from the dynamic that operates between the other
characters in her world, and second, that to participate in this dynamic has ruinous effects on
their creativity. Everything turns on the degree of investment in the visual; for it is the
presence of a gaze which generates the paranoia and the narcissism that go with social
relations – and thus brings gender into being. The only way to close the breach through which
visual, social and gendered existence comes into being is to close the gap between people. In
Sarraute it is distance that separates person from person, producing the alienating effects that
turn characters into 'characters' and destroying the creative efforts of the writer.

It is not enough for Sarraute to assume that in writing she can escape social and
gendered existence simply by believing – like the character in '*Fools say*' – in her own
invisibility. Everything depends on breaking down the distance in which visual relations
flourish and on creating a relation based on contact rather than sight. There are a great
many ways in which Sarraute seeks to create intimacy of contact, but there is one in
particular that I should like to explore here in more detail: identification.[19] It is axiomatic
in Sarraute that the inner world of the *tropism* is a universal phenomenon and it is on the
basis of this phenomenon that identification is made possible. Alain Guimier articulates
the principle with reference to his aunt, Tante Berthe, when she is dismissively
characterised by another character as 'A crank, and that's all there is to it' (pp. 31/29). Alain
responds by claiming an identification where his interlocutor sees only difference:

> 'I can't make myself believe that there is a fundamental difference between people. . . I
> always believe – perhaps it's idiotic – that somewhere beyond, everyone is alike, everyone
> resembles everyone else. . . So I don't dare judge. . . Right away I feel that I'm like them, as
> soon as I remove my carapace, this thin varnish. . .' (pp. 33/31)

'Feeling like' others is the motive force of Nathalie Sarraute's literary enterprise: at the
level of the tropism we all supposedly feel the same; the reader is persuaded of this
truth by being made to *feel like* the characters; and, finally, Sarraute herself claims her
prerogative as author on the basis of her ability, similarly, to *feel like* her characters.

In one sense, gender is made irrelevant by this pervasive identification: Alain Guimier identifies with his old aunt and readers identify with characters regardless of their sex. As Sarraute proudly records in an interview with Isabelle Huppert:

> When *The Planetarium* came out, I was interviewed by a young man who said to me: 'Oh! Tante Berthe is me. I've just got married and I get up in the night to look at the door-handles. . .' I was so pleased![20]

But in her conversations with Simone Benmussa, Sarraute comments on the process of identification in a way that suggests that gender is not totally excluded from it. In her remarks about women on the stage she argues that gender (at least in women) constitutes an obstacle to identification. And she also claims that if, in her work, she represents men as gender-neutral, this is in part the result of the demasculinising effect of her own identification with them:

> It's very strange, but when I construct my characters, I don't visualise any specifically masculine behaviour. . . Actually, I know why it is. . . it's probably because I set up a sort of counterweight whose effects mean that this behaviour never seems to me to be characteristically virile because it's also my own behaviour. It becomes neuter [*neutre*] by virtue of the fact that I participate in it, and at a stroke, I neutralise it. (p142)

It is certainly true that the central figures in the first three novels (the narrators of *Portrait of a Man Unknown* and *Martereau* and Alain Guimier in *The Planetarium*) whose function is to provide testimony to the existence of the tropism, are all lacking in conventional masculine qualities. The middle-aged male narrator of *Portrait of a Man Unknown* pales in terms of virility alongside the bluff masculinity exhibited by the Old Man or the solidly masculine virtues of the daughter's future husband, Dumontet. Similarly, in *Martereau* the narrator's uncle presents himself to the world as a man toughened by the world's knocks, and has little patience for what he regards as the airy-fairy sensibilities of his nephew. And Alain Guimier is clearly viewed by his mother-in-law as failing to conform to the masculine role she requires for her daughter's husband: insufficiently serious, lacking in foresight, apparently uninterested in a proper career, 'he's queer about certain things, he's not like other young men of his age' (*The Planetarium*, pp. 59/55). The tropisms which are Sarraute's quarry are most palpably present in men whose masculinity is least in evidence.

Yet both tropisms and the creative enterprise that depicts them are invariably sanctioned by men, not women. If it is a man in the form of the 'specialist' who comes closest to putting an end to the narrator's attempt to confirm the inner reality he senses in the Old Man and his daughter in *Portrait of a Man Unknown*, it is nevertheless another man, in the form of the 'Portrait of a Man Unknown' in the gallery in Holland, who provides the narrator with the conviction that the inner life exists and so frees him from the specialist's embargo. This is brought about through an experience of identification that breaks down the distance between the narrator and the painted subject: what counts is not what the Unknown Man in the portrait *looks like*, but what he makes the narrator *feel like*:

> And little by little, I became aware that a timid note, an almost forgotten strain from long
> ago, had sounded within me, at first hesitantly. And it seemed to me, as I stood there before
> him, dissolved in him, that this faltering, frail note, this timid response he had awakened in
> me, penetrated him and reverberated inside him, that he seized it and gave it back to me
> increased and magnified as though by an amplifier; it began to rise from me and from him,
> louder and louder, a song filled with hope that lifted me up and bore me along. . .[21]

Moreover, this is a somewhat bizarre form of identification since it reverses the usual
direction of identification in art where the reader or spectator identifies with the
represented character. Here, curiously, it is the painted subject who ends up *feeling like*
the narrator, returning the narrator's intuitions to him in magnified and amplified
confirmation of them, rather than vice versa. The point, however, lies precisely in the
confirmation that this reverse identification brings.

   This scene takes place within Sarraute's fiction but there are important ways in
which Sarraute stages her own literary enterprise within a context that is validated by
men. On a personal level, she claims that it was her husband who encouraged her to
write. When she began *Tropisms* in 1932, 'he understood immediately what I was trying
to do'. Moreover, his responses as a reader of her work are invoked by her as a
guarantee of its validity. Sarraute read everything she wrote to her husband Raymond
Sarraute and when she did so 'I would know at once what worked and what didn't.'
Because, 'As I read to him, we would have the same responses.' When Raymond
Sarraute died in 1985, Sarraute found herself for the first time without someone to
whom she could read her work 'who would react *like me*'.[22]

   From a less personal and more literary-historical perspective, Sarraute also seeks
to validate her work through a series of male identifications. In the preface to *The
Age of Suspicion* she speaks of a need she feels to understand her place in the
evolution of the novel by examining the works of other writers 'in an effort to
discover an irreversible direction in literature that would permit me to see if my
own quest was in line with this direction'.[23] In one sense it is hardly surprising if
almost all the examples she chooses are the works of men, since neither French nor
Russian literature (her main points of reference) contain many examples of women
writers. But Sarraute is doing more than map a field or write a history, and her own
writing is presented as having a particular form of relation to precursor texts that is
almost always grounded in a form of projective identification which turns her own
texts into continuations of the work of her male precursors.

   The prime example of this is Dostoevsky, whose *Brothers Karamazov* is not so
much analysed as rewritten by Sarraute in her essay 'From Dostoievski to
Kafka'. In Sarraute's rendering, his characters become rather like the Unknown
Man in the portrait, agents of 'a timid. . . appeal', and incarnations of 'a way of
showing that they are quite near, accessible, disarmed, open, acquiescent, in
complete surrender, completely abandoned to the understanding, the generosity
of the other' (pp. 72/43-4). She concludes her discussion of Dostoevsky by
claiming that behind the apparent variations of characters and temperaments in
his work, it is possible to discern 'a sort of new unanimism' (pp. 76/53) – an

assertion which inscribes her 'tropisms' within the work of her precursor and presents her own as a continuation of it.

There is a similar – if in some senses more daring – move in relation to Tolstoy in *Portrait of a Man Unknown*. Tolstoy offers less propitious material than Dostoevsky for the sort of vision that Sarraute is seeking to present as part of a continuous evolution. Indeed, in an article in *Les Lettres françaises*, she contrasts the two Russian writers to the detriment of Tolstoy whom she dismissively characterises as the novelist of socially consecrated appearances.[24] But here, in her first novel, she wrests a tender concession to her own perception of things out of the curmudgeonly Prince Bolkonski, as she has him whisper 'douchenka' to his daughter on his deathbed, thus implicitly attesting to the existence of

> a thousand extremely fine and barely discernible threads – here we have again the trembling, sticky gossamer threads – [which] must have emanated continually from Princess Marie to cling to him, and eventually envelop him. (pp .66/69)

These are precisely the ties that the narrator imagines bind the daughter to the Old Man in *Portrait of a Man Unknown* and are the stuff of the psychology of Sarraute's tropisms. And it is perhaps no more fanciful than Sarraute's own supposition about Prince Bolkonski to imagine that Tolstoy – just as curmudgeonly as his gruff Prince – is being made to concede that the writing of his honorary daughter is bringing to light the hidden psychological truths that lie behind the 'hard, closed mask' of his characters.[25]

Portrait of a Man Unknown is also a rewriting of Balzac's *Eugénie Grandet* insofar as it is – at least at a superficial level – the story of a miser and his daughter. And it was first published with a preface by Sartre which gave it yet another sort of male blessing.[26] Sartre makes no explicit reference to Sarraute's sex, and says nothing to suggest that there is anything characteristically feminine about the novel he is presenting to the public. Instead, he sets Sarraute's work in a constellation of male references: Nabokov, Evelyn Waugh, Gide, Roger Caillois, Rousseau, Dostoevsky, Meredith, Rembrandt, Miro, Heidegger and so on. And he concludes by describing the book as 'difficult' and 'excellent', terms which do not have ready feminine connotations. (Beauvoir in *The Second Sex,* published the following year, was, as we have seen, to suggest that women's writing was more likely to be conventional and mediocre than difficult and excellent.) In these various ways, then, Sarraute can be seen to stage her entry as a novelist into the literary world under the sponsorship of men.

References to women writers in her work are few and far between. The allusion to Katherine Mansfield is only fleeting; Mme de Lafayette is mentioned on a few occasions but always in association with the male Benjamin Constant and always as an example of an outmoded tradition of psychological analysis. Virginia Woolf is the only woman writer whom Sarraute quotes at any length (in her critical essay 'Conversation and Sub-conversation'). But any suggestion that Sarraute and Woolf might resemble each other in any way is met with assertions of radical differences between the two on Sarraute's part. In an interview in 1961, Sarraute was asked what she thought of the comparison that had been made between her work and that of Woolf and her reply does everything to maximise a contrast:

> People have talked about the 'similarities' between us, and about the influence of Virginia Woolf on what I've written. I think our sensibilities are really the opposite of each other. In Virginia Woolf, the entire universe, mobilised by time, flows through the consciousnesses of the characters, who are passive and as if swept hither and thither by the endless flow of moments.
>
> In my work the characters are always in a state of hyperactivity: there's a dramatic action being played out at the level of their 'tropisms', those rapid movements on the edge of consciousness. And that produces a completely different stylistic rhythm.[27]

This response from Sarraute uses every means at her disposal to prevent readers and critics from assimilating the two women writers with each other, thus limiting the possibility of constructing Sarraute's work as an example of women's writing.

Every mention by Sarraute of her mother's writing similarly emphasises the difference between the two ('the way she wrote was the opposite of me, with great facility and much joy');[28] and any allusion to Simone de Beauvoir always elicits the most oppositional response from Sarraute. She holds Beauvoir (and not Sartre) reponsible for the cuts imposed on her first critical essay, 'Paul Valéry et l'Enfant d'Éléphant' which appeared in *Les Temps modernes* in 1947, and also for the same journal's rejection of her essay 'Conversation and Sub-conversation' in 1955.[29] And despite a brief friendship between the two women in the late 40s, there appears to have been no love lost between them: Beauvoir wrote a hostile account of Sarraute's fiction in *Force of Circumstance*,[30] and Sarraute's views about Beauvoir have appeared in print under the title 'Nathalie Sarraute does not want to have anything in common with Simone de Beauvoir'.[31] For all the common cause one may discern between the two on the issue of gender, Sarraute is interested only in keeping a distance between herself and this other well-known, post-war woman writer of her generation.

If Sarraute is to succeed in writing as a human being she can do so only in the company of men and not of women, creating identifications with male precursors, and receiving from men the baton in the relay race of literary evolution.[32] But her aim is not not to wear trousers *à la* Sand and to become one of the chaps. Sarraute does not so much want to be like a man as to present herself as validated by men who are willing to admit that *they* are like *her*. Theatrical modes of being may ultimately prove inescapable, as Sarraute has recourse to a series of stagings of these identifications, grounded though they are in a non-specular form of relation. But by means of this dual manoeuvre – a staged invocation of a non-specular identification – Sarraute seeks to solve the dilemma posed for the woman writer who feels herself trapped in the gender-producing gaze of the world. As with the narrator in *Portrait of a Man Unknown* before the portrait of the Unknown Man, she projects her own voice into the work of her male precursors and, with the blessing of their identification, has them send her out into the world, delivered from the chain which binds her to her feminine condition.

1. Interview with Sonia Rykiel, *Les Nouvelles*, 9-15 February 1984, pp. 39-41 (p.40). Where no English translation of quoted material exists I have provided my own.
2. Pierre Demeron, 'Nathalie Sarraute ou la littérature sans cabotinage', *Arts*, 3-9 June 1959, p. 2.
3. Although perhaps it afforded her some indulgence: one version of the photograph shows her with her legs crossed but according to Alain Robbe-Grillet she asked to have the photo altered to show her standing with her feet apart (conversation with Robbe-Grillet in June 1994). Both versions of this famous photograph are common. See Arnaud Rykner, *Nathalie Sarraute*, Éditions du Seuil, Paris, 1991, p. 190 for a touched-up version.
4. Interview with Michèle Gazier, 'Nathalie Sarraute et son "il"', *Télérama* no. 1800, 11 July 1984, pp.38-9 (p. 38). Here she goes on to say 'and the more androgynous they are, the better', but later she will argue for 'neuter' instead of the more Woolf-ian 'androgyny'. See below. For equally trenchant comments on *écriture féminine*, see also the interview with Sonia Rykiel. There have been a number of attempts to claim Sarraute for a version of *écriture féminine*, even while acknowledging Sarraute's own resistance to the idea and the difficulty of any simple reclamation of Sarraute to a contemporary feminist cause. See for example, the two book-length studies, Sarah Barbour, *Nathalie Sarraute and the Feminist Reader: Identities in Process*, Associated University Presses, London and Toronto, 1993; John Phillips, *Nathalie Sarraute: Metaphor, Fairy-Tale and the Feminine of the Text*, Peter Lang, Washington, D.C., 1994.
5. Interview with Michèle Gazier, p. 38.
6. 'At Fénélon [the girl's *lycée* she attended] very few girls went in for the *baccalauréat*,' recalls Nathalie Sarraute in an interview. The men teachers who came from boys' *lycées* to teach some of the top classes were very different from the women teachers she was used to: 'There was a huge difference from the teachers we'd have before, who had been trained at Sèvres [the girls' section of the École Normale Supérieure] and who had a completely different way of teaching.' Interview with Danièle Salenave, 'Sur la langue, l'écriture, le travail', *Genesis* no. 5, 1994, pp. 117-21 (pp. 117-18). For a full and very sobering discussion of the nature and extent of the differences between the education of girls and of their teachers at the École Normale Supérieure for women at Sèvres, as compared to their male counterparts, see Toril Moi, *Simone de Beauvoir: The Making of an Intellectual Woman*, Blackwell, Oxford, 1994, esp. Chapter 2.
7. Simone de Beauvoir, *The Second Sex* (1949), translated by H.M. Parshley, London, Jonathan Cape, p.273. I have quoted the English translations of French texts where these exist, but altered them where it seemed necessary. Page references in the text are to the cited English version, followed by one to the French version – in this case, *Le deuxième sexe*, Gallimard, Idées, Paris, 1968, vol. I, p. 285.
8. *Nathalie Sarraute: Qui êtes-vous?*, Conversations with Simone Benmussa, La Manufacture, Lyon, 1987, p. 142. Sarraute invokes the notion of 'the neuter' (*le neutre*) to define the gender status of the 'human being'.
9. Monique Wittig has made a strong case for the eradication of gender in writing and mentions the example of Sarraute whose work 'while being of another nature' nevertheless inspired some of the strategies of her own writing. See 'The Mark of Gender', in *The Poetics of Gender*, edited by Nancy K. Miller, Columbia University Press, New York, 1986, pp. 63-73 (p.73).
10. '*Fools say*', translated by Maria Jolas, John Calder, London, 1977, p. 28 / '*disent les imbéciles*', Gallimard, Paris, 1976, p. 35.
11. Blurb from the Gallimard edition. From *The Planetarium* onwards, Sarraute has always written her own blurbs.
12. Pp. 62 / 69. The published translation gives 'it' for 'she' since Sarraute is personifying an 'idea', which in French is a female noun. The fact that the personification as a woman is possible says a great deal about the terms in which the 'image of woman' functions in Sarraute's world.
13. See interview with François-Marie Banier in *Le Monde des livres*, 15 April 1983, p. 13.
14. *Childhood*, translated by Barbara Wright, John Calder, London, 1984, p. 82 / *Enfance*, Gallimard, Paris, 1983, p. 91. Kolya was Sarraute's mother's second husband.
15. This key phrase comes from Katherine Mansfield's *Journal* and is used in Sarraute's essays in *The Age of Suspicion*.
16. Interview with François-Marie Banier, p. 13.
17. *The Planetarium*, translated by Maria Jolas, John Calder, London, 1961, p. 91 / *Le Planétarium*, Gallimard, Paris, 1959, p. 83.
18. *The Planetarium*, pp. 175-6. The gesture in *Childhood* is described as follows: 'I can't remember her looking at herself in the mirror, powedering her face. . . only her rapid glance when she passed a looking glass, and her hasty gesture to push a stray wisp of hair back into her bun, push in a protruding pin. . .' (pp.82/91).

19. I have examined some of these strategies for creating contact elsewhere: 'Criticism and the Terrible Desire to Establish Contact' (*L'Esprit créateur*, vol. XXXVI, no. 2, 1996, pp. 44-62) looks at the role of Sarraute's critical writings in creating this contact and the function of certain literary techniques in her writing as a means of sustaining it; 'Materialism and the Mind: Nathalie Sarraute' (*Romance Studies*, no. 20, 1992, pp. 31-43) explores the role played by the body in Sarraute as the basis for an appeal to a common experience; and, 'Différences et Différends chez Nathalie Sarraute' (in *Nathalie Sarraute: Un écrivain dans le siècle*, forthcoming) considers some of the ways in which difference is perceived in Sarraute as the source of a catastrophic breach between subjects.

20. Interview with Isabelle Huppert, 'Rencontre: Nathalie Sarraute', *Cahiers du Cinéma*, no. 177, March 1994, pp. 8-14 (p. 10).

21. *Portrait of a Man Unknown*, translated by Maria Jolas, John Calder, London, 1959, p. 85 / *Portrait d'un inconnu*, Gallimard, Paris, 1957, p. 87. Naomi Schor makes some interesting remarks about this passage in her essay 'The Portrait of a Gentleman: Representing Men in (French) Women's Writing' in *Bad Objects: Essays Popular and Unpopular*, Duke University Press, Durham NC, 1995, pp. 111-31. In particular she notes that this 'curious form of mutual resonance . . . bypasses the specular in favour of the vocal' (p. 130).

22. *Nathalie Sarraute: Qui êtes-vous?*, pp. 151-2, my emphasis.

23. Foreword to *Tropisms and The Age of Suspicion*, translated by Maria Jolas, John Calder, London, 1963, p.10. This Foreword is dated Paris 1962, and an expanded version of it was included in the second edition of *L'Ère du soupçon*, published in Gallimard's 'Idées' series in 1964. The same comments appear in the French edition on p. 10.

24. Nathalie Sarraute, 'Tolstoï', *Les Lettres françaises*, no. 842, 22-28 September 1960, pp. 1,5.

25. In *L'Usage de la parole* (Paris, Gallimard, 1980), Sarraute stages another deathbed scene in which she picks up the words of the dying Chekhov, amplifies them and gives them resonance, so that he too ends up being 'like her'. See 'Ich sterbe'.

26. *Portrait d'un inconnu (Portrait of a Man Unknown)* was first published by Robert Marin in Paris in 1948 with a preface by Sartre. This preface has become a quasi-integral part of Sarraute's text, appearing in every published version, and included even in the Pléiade *Œuvres complètes*. This would seem to suggest that Sarraute has actively acquiesced in Sartre's public sanctioning of her writing

27. Nathalie Sarraute, 'Virginia Woolf ou la visionnaire du maintenant', *Les Lettres françaises*, no. 882, 29 June - 5 July 1961, pp. 1,3 (p. 3).

28. Interview in *Le Monde*, 15 April 1983, p.13.

29. See notes to both these essays in Nathalie Sarraute, *Œuvres Complètes*, Bibliothèque de la Pléiade, Paris, Gallimard, 1996.

30. Translated by Richard Howard, André Deutsch and Weidenfeld and Nicolson, London, 1965, pp. 271-2 / *La Force des choses*, Gallimard, 1963, p. 291.

31. In this interview with Thérèse de Saint Phalle, Sarraute comments on Beauvoir's latest novel, *Les Belles Images*, as follows: 'I've read Simone de Beauvoir's novel. It's impossible for me to see the *slightest* connection between her book and my books. There isn't a single thing in common! Neither in the form, nor in the content!' *Le Figaro littéraire*, 5 January 1967, p. 10.

32. The metaphor of the relay race for literary evolution is implied in much of Sarraute's critical writing and is made explicit in an interview published under the title 'Où va le roman?' in *Le Canada français*, no. 34, 1961, pp. 161-72: 'I believe that each of us comes after others, each of us has precursors, and that literature is a relay race where the writer hands on the baton to the person who comes after' (p. 163).

Dennis The Menace?: Hegemonic Masculinity And Dennis Potter's *The Singing Detective*

Maroula Joannou[1]

Television drama which has been successful in reaching mass audiences and receiving critical acclaim has been a relatively recent and peculiarly British phenomenon. In many European countries, including France, Italy, Germany and Spain, in which there are lively, popular and well-established theatrical traditions, innovative contemporary drama has tended to be almost exclusively the preserve of the theatre. There has been no European equivalent of the high-quality television drama associated in Britain with writers like Alan Bleasdale and Jack Rosenthal, and especially with Dennis Potter, whose 30-year writing career, beginning just before the two Nigel Barton plays in 1965, has been largely synonymous with the history and development of British television drama itself.

The subject of much of Potter's writing for television has been sexual violence, most famously in *Brimstone and Treacle*, made in 1976 but banned by the BBC for ten years, in which a brain-damaged girl is raped by the devil. But it is also present in other well-known works including *Pennies from Heaven* (1978), in which a beautiful blind young woman is sexually assaulted and murdered; *The Singing Detective* (1986), in which the bodies of several naked women are dredged up from the Thames; *Black Eyes* (1989), in which a young model is exploited by her uncle and by the sex industry; and *Lipstick On Your Collar* (1993), in which a woman is assaulted and sexually abused by her husband. The purpose of this essay is to provide a feminist critique of Potter's classic television series *The Singing Detective* (1986). I wish to analyse how desire in *The Singing Detective* has been masculinised, made dependent on the dichotomies of self-and-other, subject and object, in which the illicit secrets and fantasies of heterosexual masculinity are projected onto women.

By the time of his death in 1994 Potter's reputation as one of the great innovators and experimentalists of British television had been securely established. As John Naughtan put it, 'nobody before or since has understood the grammar of television as well as Potter, or used it to such powerful effect'.[2] A consistently outspoken opponent of naturalism ('as though all that out there, all that is beyond your view, is solidly defined by some kind of consensus as to what it is. So that the 'truth' is that out there and all you have to do is show it'),[3] the high point of Potter's dramatic achievement was reached with *The Singing Detective*. This starred Michael Gambon in the role of Philip Marlow[4] and was broadcast in November 1986 to both critical and popular acclaim – Chris Dunckley of *The Financial Times* describing the series as 'probably the most compelling piece of original television fiction that I have seen in 16 years as a critic'.[5]

The Singing Detective represented a powerful assault upon the 'narrative tyranny'[6] of television. It demonstrated the untapped potential of visual excess and the power of cinematic camera and editing techniques – a power to produce a non-naturalistic narrative that resonated with meaning far beyond what the narration of the familiar linear television drama was able to express. The six-part series deployed many strategies usually associated with the *avant-garde* but at the same time it embraced the popular appeal of detective fiction, the television 'sitcom', the hospital drama and the music of the 'big band' era, and attracted a peak audience of eight million.

Dennis Potter's status as Britain's first television 'auteur' had not come about accidentally but had been actively promoted by his supporters in the BBC. As Rosalind Coward had observed in 1978, a 'hidden agenda' had existed inside the Corporation whereby the new, more liberal, regime in power during the late 1970s was enabled to mark a distance from its predecessors by making clear its commitment to a controversial writer whose withering invective and sexual explicitness were often designed to shock:[7] 'Potter was in many ways the Jonathan Swift of his time. He was very aware of the follies of mankind and he could use the rhetoric of disgust as strongly in interviews and journalism as in his screenplays.'[8] For much of the 1980s, as Paul Giles has pointed out, the Corporation was intent on safeguarding its editorial independence from a Conservative government which had vituperatively criticised its policies.[9] At the same time, the massive national audiences for television drama meant that television attracted talented, ambitious writers who understood its potential as a public arena in which the political could be vigorously contested.[10] Thus, as Lester Friedman has observed, 'the intense and unwavering hatred of Margaret Thatcher in the 1980s provided the spark necessary to force Britain's best visual artists to new creative heights'.[11]

Interviewed shortly before his death, Potter articulated many of his most deeply-held convictions, including his support for the 1945 Labour government as 'one of the great governments of British history', his unwavering belief in the welfare state, and his undisguised contempt for Margaret Thatcher and John Major, whom he held personally responsible for its wanton demolition.[12] As an outspoken critic of the BBC's John Birt and the newspaper magnate Rupert Murdoch, Potter had not only come to be strongly identified with the political opposition to Thatcherism but also to be widely regarded as a figurehead for progressive elements within the worlds of broadcasting and the media.

In view of Potter's untimely death and the widespread respect for his inventiveness and versatility as a writer, it is hardly surprising that critics have been prepared to overlook, if not to exonerate, the attitudes to women in his writing for television to which I want to draw attention. Foremost among his defenders is John R. Cook who sees Potter's depiction of female characters as either madonnas and magdalenes as merely a reflection of 'Western society's traditional way of looking at women', arguing that in the process of 'dramatising what goes on inside his male characters' heads,

Potter is ultimately investigating the nature of patriarchy itself and how men have traditionally been taught to view women'.[13] However, Cook's argument is undermined by the fact that Potter himself had never denied his own misogyny. When questioned explicitly on the subject by Graham Fuller he attributed its presence to the residual influence on him of traditional working-class attitudes, 'if you come up with English working-class male ideas about women then traces of that – no, more than traces – a lot of that is going to cling to you for a long time'.[14] Moreover, Potter's biographer, Stephen W. Gilbert, quotes the dramatist's reply to the producer Gareth Davies who put it to Potter that all his women characters were ' "somebody's mother, or somebody's wife or somebody's mistress, that's all they're there for, to serve some sort of male". "That's right", he said. "All my own fantasies".'[15]

I shall use the notion of hegemonic masculinity to argue that *The Singing Detective* is heavily reliant on reductive and demeaning images of women and that the series trades on voyeuristic fantasies that provide pleasure for male audiences. But the aesthetics of television are complex. While much of television drama simply reproduces the common societal assumptions about gender, it may also encourage the viewer to reflect back upon them. To use an analogy taken from the theatre, it is possible for any critic to argue either that Othello, Lear and Hamlet are all motivated by misogynistic attitudes to women or, equally plausibly, that Shakespeare has demonstrated the murderous folly of the foolish idealisation of women, as is shown through the fate of Desdemona, Cordelia and Ophelia. To put it simply, Potter's defence against charges of misogyny in *The Singing Detective* might be to argue that the series offers a critique of the symptomatic assumptions under which the character Philip Marlow labours. The critic Peter Stead has contended that 'the emphasis on sexual abuse, guilt and anxiety in his [Potter's] work is rooted in his own experience and must be taken as serious comment on issues and phenomena that for decades society as a whole has chosen to ignore.'[16]

As I have said, desire in *The Singing Detective* is masculinised, predicated upon the dichotomies of self-and-other, subject-and-object, in which the secrets and fantasies of masculinity are projected onto women. It is important to distinguish between masculinity, the social and cultural expectations which regulate the behaviour and attitudes of men in general, and hegemonic masculinity, which is a question of 'how particular men inhabit positions of power and wealth and how they legitimate and reproduce social relationships that generate dominance'.[17]

Hegemonic masculinity defines the dominance of a particular variety or notion of masculinity that prescribes what it means to be a 'proper' man, thus securing the ascendancy of particular men and the subordination of women, within the hierarchical ordering of the gender system.[18] As Robert Hanke has argued, 'hegemonic masculinity thus works through a variety of representational strategies, including images of effeminised masculinity and the construction of negative symbols of masculinity, in order to win the consent of male and female viewers, who, as social agents, may be situated differently'.[19]

While much of television has assumed the male point of view to be normative and has taken women and images of women as its object of scrutiny, it has seldom investigated men and the male image in the same way. There is, therefore, an important sense in which the images and functions of heterosexual masculinity within television have been left undiscussed, with the result that questions of power and sexual inequality have also remained unaddressed. As Andy Metcalf and Martin Humphries put it, 'it is true that much male thinking is infused with misogyny – but that is neither unchanging nor immutable. Beneath the mask of manly resolve there is all too often a chaotic state of conflict and ambivalence. But there is nothing inevitable about this.'[20] On the contrary, desire itself is socially constructed and sexual desire is shaped by social structures, institutions and representations, and as such feminists would argue that it can be contested and changed. Moreover, the virulently misogynistic representations of women as *femmes fatales*, which I shall identify in *The Singing Detective*, are predicated on a denial of what men know to be true – that sex is not unproblematic but is beset with complications and anxieties – of impotence, ineptness and inadequacy – and that any kind of dialogue, 'establishing and developing the emotional contexts and needs which both women and men bring to their sex lives, has been conspicuous in its absence'[21] both in *The Singing Detective* and in Potter's writing career as a whole.

The institutional and production context of *The Singing Detective* has been helpfully discussed by both John R. Cook and Joost Hunnigher[22] and need not detain us here. But the construction of the main character in *The Singing Detective* is crucially important to an understanding of the representations of masculinity and femininity in the television series. Philip Marlow is introduced from the very beginning as a chronic sufferer from psoriatic arthritis, a disease affecting the skin and joints, which has aggravated his decidedly jaundiced outlook on the world. As Potter puts it, Marlow 'was stripped of everything: he had no faith in himself; no belief in any political, religious or social system; he was full of a witty despair and cynicism'.[23] Instead of the confident manifestations of masculinity to which we have become accustomed on screen, *The Singing Detective* offers the spectacle of a sick man in hospital living out his sexual identity in neurotic, disturbed, introspective and psychotic ways. As Marlow, a writer of pulp fiction, undergoes treatment, he imaginatively enacts the leading role in his own detective thriller, *The Singing Detective*. His wartime childhood in the Forest of Dean is also dramatised. In place of a body that is active and whole, *The Singing Detective* offers a male body which is hideously disfigured. The skin is cracked, scabbed, scaled and swollen, an object of shock to his fellow patients, of pity to the viewer and of clinical curiosity to the physician.

The spectacle of Marlowe's deformed and ailing body signifies a rupture of the usual relationship between the male body and the cultural power. Kaja Silverman has described this: 'Male subjectivity is a kind of stress point, the juncture at which social crisis and turmoil frequently find most dramatic expression.' Major rifts between the dominant fiction and the larger social formation can almost always be detected within a classic narrative film through the breakdown of sexual difference – through the disclosure of male lack or impotence.[24]

To compensate for his physical disfigurement Marlow has been forced to become stridently masculine, to disown the femininity inside him. Marlowe's hatred of women springs from his own supposed feminine qualities and the ensuing desire to destroy them. To make women detestable is his way of destroying femininity and that includes the hatred of that inside himself which is potentially feminine, vulnerable and powerless.

Marlow is presented to the cameras as a sacrificial figure, wearing only a loincloth, like Jesus on the cross, filmed from above in a *film-noir* extreme high long-shot, an oppressive and fatalistic angle that looks down on its helpless victim laid out like a fish on a slab. Reduced to a state of abject passivity, although mentally agile, Marlowe's feminised appearance is underscored by his long, dishevelled hair. The camera emphasises his inability to stand upright as he lies horizontally, helpless and stranded in his hospital bed.

In her study of the Yorkshire Ripper, *The Streetcleaner: The Yorkshire Ripper Case on Trial*, Nicole Ward Jouve has suggested that the ability to stand upright is indicative of masculinity and that the prone or 'Sleeping Beauty' position bespeaks femininity.[25] Richard Dyer, too, has observed that 'straining and striving are the terms most often used to describe male sexuality in this society' and that images of men must disavow passivity 'if they are to be kept in line with dominant ideas of masculinity-as-activity'.[26] Unable to walk, and forced to ask the nurse for the bedpan, Marlow is infantilised; forbidden cigarettes and instead offered sweets, he regresses into a condition of complete dependency.

Later, in a classically feminine position, Marlow lies passively in bed while his body is manipulated. He tries to prevent the visible manifestation of his masculinity, an erection ('Oh cock do not crow') – and the pain and pleasure in the erotic, mildly sado-masochistic sequences between patient and nurse are similar to rubbing iodine in a cut (episode 1).

In the beginning, *The Singing Detective* has all the hallmarks of an anti-psychiatric drama like *Family Life* or *One Flew Over the Cuckoo's Nest*. The medical/psychiatric authorities appear intent on depriving the patient of all remnants of dignity. The imperious consultant enters to the music of the Queen of Sheba (episode 1). The wide-angle lens causes the faces of the medical team to bulge forward ominously as they loom over Marlow, inviting the viewer to understand, and even to share, his sense of terror and persecution.

From Marlowe's point of view the medical team appears in an intimidatory, hallucinatory fashion, resembling a mock-Greek chorus which towers over him, intoning chants of librium, valium and anti-depressants. His humour helps him to diffuse the tension and reduce them to size. Marlow mutters that he will find equanimity only after they have 'finally turned me into a potato' (episode 1). He is reminded of being a baby in his pram 'being drooled over by slobbering cretins' who 'thought they were doctors and nurses' but who 'turned out to be escapees from the local loony bin' (episode 1).

But the later episodes take on the character of a psychoanalytic voyage of discovery which brings to the surface submerged areas of memory, trauma and suppressed fear. The breakdown of Marlowe's resistance to a 'talking cure' sets him on the road to recovery. As he admits his guilt on discovering that a boy for whose punishment he was responsible has spent years in a mental institution, the camera no longer allows his therapist to dominate Marlow but patient and consultant are filmed in shot-reverse-shot as equals. Marlow then lifts himself out of his wheelchair to the Inkspots/Ella Fitzgerald version of 'Into Each Life Some Rain Must Fall'.

The women in *The Singing Detective* are those from Marlowe's childhood, those whom he meets as an adult and those whom he invents in his detective fiction. They are the projections of Marlowe's consciousness and the dynamics of simultaneous attraction and repulsion. Marlow is an inveterate misanthropist, hating the human species as a whole, directing insults at the medical team and the Asian patient in an adjoining bed (episode 1). His misogyny is part of this wider misanthropy and his enmity shifts away from the universe at large and is directed specifically at women.

One possible cause of misogynistic behaviour in men is the combination of a passive father and a dominating mother. Like many misogynists Marlow unconsciously hates his mother and projects that hatred onto other women. His fear of the feminine within himself also arises from his troubled relationship with his father, a likeable but flawed model of working-class masculinity who resembles Potter's own father, a miner in the Forest of Dean exempted from military service in the Second World War ('he was shy, he was gentle, he was a bit feckless in many ways').[27]

The boy's father makes desultory and ineffectual attempts to assert his authority during the breakdown of his marriage. But he is unable to prove himself a man in the traditional way by providing adequately for his family, and he becomes the butt of his wife's anger at being made to live in an isolated hovel. At best an ambivalent model of working-class manhood, he loves Philip with his 'whole heart' and the boy, who clutches his father's hand tightly after his mother's death, obviously returns that love (episode 6).

Mrs Marlow, like Eve, is responsible for the loss of Eden through her wilful disobedience. The primal scene between the boy's mother and her lover, Raymond Binney, takes place in the woods, hitherto associated exclusively with Philip and emblematic of the innocence of childhood. The woman is splayed out on the ground and burdened with the weight of the male body. The camera is identified with Binney as it zooms in to focus on her breasts. The man's interest in the woman appears purely carnal. Binney bites her breasts and mauls her body. She bursts into tears afterwards, perhaps signifying shame at having consented to being reduced to nothing more than her bodily functions (episode 3).

As John Ellis has noted, the distinction between voyeurism and fetishistic looking implies in the latter the direct acknowledgment and participation of the object viewed with the fetishistic attitude, the compliant look of the character directed towards the viewer.[28] As Mrs Marlow sits tearfully in the railway carriage going to London, she is surrounded by admiring soldiers and applies bright red lipstick as the camera dwells on parts of her body. She refuses a cigarette from a soldier who comments, 'no vices, eh.' Her ambivalent response is, 'I wouldn't bank on it' (episode 3).

The boy is able to sense that her mother's attractiveness to other men poses a threat to his father's status. Philip deeply resents the veiled sexual interest that underlies the soldiers' protective overtures. When a soldier tries to comfort her he bursts out protectively, 'doosn't thou touch her. Keep thee hands off our Mum. I shall tell our Dad' (episode 3).

The boy blames his mother for his loss of innocence and banishment to the city. The first intimation of his corrosive disfigurement is a psoriatic lesion, a red and silvery white patch which appears at the same time as the boy accuses his mother of adultery. Marlowe's disease is emblematic of his disgust with sex and his anger at his mother's betrayal.

Soon after, her body is fished out of the Thames. As Elisabeth Bronfen has pointed out, 'the paradox inherent in suicide is that it can either disintegrate identity or reaffirm a woman's autonomy after defilement or abandonment'. She suggests, moreover, that 'suicide is a revitalising self-assertion in death against the lethal self-alienation in life'.[29] Abandoned by his mother, the impressionable boy finds it impossible to trust any woman again: 'Don't trust anybody again! Don't give your love. Hide in yourself. Or else they'll die. They'll die. And they'll hurt you! Hide! Hide!' (episode 6). In a game of word associations Marlow replies 'pretence' in response to 'passion' and 'fuck' in response to 'woman'. To 'fuck' he responds 'dirt'. He adds 'death' to 'dirt' (episode 5). This order perfectly replicates the events leading to his mother's suicide.

The critic Frank Krutnik has argued that 'the methodology of psychoanalysis bears similarities to processes of detection, in that the analyst seeks to bring to the surface and make visible that which is hidden or latent, unearthing concealed motivations and seeking to construct an ordered picture of the truth from a disordered and at times seemingly chaotic bricolage of clues'.[30] The psychiatrist and the singing detective are both investigative agents whose task is to expose and eradicate the deviance represented by the manipulative, sexually alluring woman and to bring about the restitution of the patriarchal order. But the eradication of deviance provides ample opportunities to indulge male voyeuristic fantasy. The advertisement for the video-tape shows a flimsily dressed woman in high heels under a lamp-post. This may, of course, be taken to be a pastiche of the covers of 1940s gangster fiction and hence to present an implicit critique of such representations.

Marlowe's paranoia leads him to believe that his wife is plotting to steal the rights to his thriller and, because Nicola is merely one of several *femmes fatales* who return to torment his imagination, she must die. Hers is one of the bodies washed up in the Thames. The psychotherapist who confronts Marlow ('You don't like women?') (episode 2) expresses surprise that he could 'so exactly duplicate such a traumatic event in your life' in the pages of fiction (episode 6).

It is out of deep self-hatred that Marlow has turned against women who fall into three categories: the sadist/torturer, the *femme fatale*, the 'angel'/virgin. The torturers include Nurse White, who insists that he says 'please' before allowing him his tea and handles his body roughly causing him pain, and Mrs Adams, the wife of an elderly patient, who assaults her husband, loudly declaiming 'it's the only way, sister. Give him one'. (episode two). But the most sadistic is the schoolteacher who publicly humiliated young Philip ('You do know that you will have to have the Big Stick. You do know that you will have to have it across your behind, and in front of the whole school') (episode 5) making him incriminate an innocent boy after he himself has defecated on the teacher's desk. Talking patriotically about freedom and Empire the old woman uses interrogation techniques, alternating between kindness and terror, reminiscent of the Gestapo, and becomes associated with Hitler in the image of the scarecrow that takes on the features of the Fuhrer and the schoolteacher in turn.

The second type of woman is the *femme fatale*. As Mary Ann Doane has noted, 'the *femme fatale* is the figure of a certain discursive unease, a potential epistemological trauma'[31] who harbours a threat which is not entirely legible, predictable, or manageable. The agonised and complex psyche of Marlow finds its echoes in the enigmatic characterisation of the women implicated in unspecified duplicity and intrigue. The 'good-time girls' at Skinscape's are alluring but potentially dangerous. Their social origins are concealed and uncertain. Amanda's speech is a 1940s nightclub concoction, affectedly American with traces of working-class London and digressions into upper-class Mayfair.

To the misogynist all women are potential prostitutes. Like the serial killer who claimed that God ordered him to cleanse the streets of prostitutes, Marlow loses the ability to discriminate between women who demand money for sex and those who do not. Peter Sutcliffe's 13 victims (and seven attempted ones) included women who were not prostitutes but this became immaterial to him: 'But he was able to tell they were prostitutes by the way they walked. He knew they were not innocent.'[32]

Women who stray outside the safe familial structures in *The Singing Detective* are depicted in terms of their desirable but destructive sexuality. Like the temptress Circe, they stand in the way of the man's progress and may have to be killed for him to win his freedom. A glamorously metamorphosed Nurse Mills turns into the singer Carlotta at Skinscape's (episode 1). Marlowe's wife photographed in the grass being made love to by an unidentified man becomes associated with his mother (episode 2). Mrs Marlow and the mysterious fur-wrapped blonde who sings *Lili Marlene* are played by the same actress (episode 3).

As Potter has put it, men 'blame women because that's the source of their unease and their wistfulness and their sexual tension. That's traditional male language. You blame it on the temptress, in religious culture the unclean vessel. But of course it's coming from the man.'[33] This would seem to indicate that the misogyny in the series exists at an implicit, conscious level and is not merely symptomatic. The damaged male often has a need to debase the woman- or mother-figure, a phenomenon described by Freud in 'On the Universal Tendency to Debasement in the Sphere of Love' (1912).[34] But because a man's sexual desire reminds him of his baser nature, it follows that all women are evil and unclean. As a consequence of his early traumas, Marlow has come to regard sexual intercourse with fear and distaste, even loathing: The question 'doesn't it disgust you, what you do?' (episode 5) ostensibly addressed to Sonia of Skinscape's is really directed at himself. When he finds himself insulting her he apologises: 'It wasn't really me calling you names. I don't mean them, I don't want to do it' (ibid). In a lurid passage in his thriller Marlow has written: 'Faces contort and stretch into a helpless leer, organs spurt out smelly stains and sticky betrayals. This is the sweaty farce out of which we are brought into being' (episode 2).

The equation between Eros and Thanatos is made explicit when a patient dies of a cardiac arrest as he describes his wartime sexual exploits in Hamburg. The scene shifts from the man's dying convulsions to the sexual intercourse in the woods which, from the boy's incredulous perspective, seems akin to violence or a physical attack (episode 3).

The third category of woman in *The Singing Detective* is the 'angel/virgin' who is represented by Nurse Mills. As Jane Selvege has noted, angels, battle-axes and sex symbols are the three groups into which most of common images of nurses fall: 'The good nurse does not complain but accepts with grace and composure everything thrown at her (or him) and self-sacrifice is shown as a virtue.'[35] Nurse Mills is young, innocent and beautiful. Never having heard of his boozing, brawling, literary namesake, she poses no intellectual challenge to Marlow. Dressed in virginal white and lacking his wife's sexual sophistication (Nicola wears flamboyant red and black), she poses no sexual threat to him either. Nurse Mills refuses to display anger or to appear ruffled. Unconscious of her sexual appeal to Marlow, she tries hard not to hurt him as she massages his body. 'By far the nicest person' that Marlow has 'met in a long time', she is an idealised figure, the 'girl in all those songs' (episode 6).

But, as Selvege also points out, angels, unless rescued by marriage, have a habit of ageing into battle-axes and 'the dedication which is depicted so charmingly in the soft young nurse turns into fanaticism' in her middle-aged counterparts who 'turn sour and vent their frustrations in petty tyranny'.[36] The night-nurse is negligent and uncooperative. Asleep on duty, she does not hear a patient's cries for the bedpan and when she does bestir herself she appears excessively disgruntled. Instead of helping Marlow she humiliates him by bursting into laughter. I have argued that the onset of Marlowe's disease is emblematic of his disgust with the physical processes of sex and his anger at his mother's betrayal. At one level the illness is a metaphor for his misogyny, for the hatred of the female characters whom he has allowed to get 'under his skin'. But Marlow also has a strong investment in his illness. As his physician puts it,' others who are just as bad and worse do not react to their condition in quite the same way. They do not rail against the world and all that is in it. They do not behave as though they have fallen into a sewer' (episode 1). The psoriasis, then, is to some extent psychosomatic, an outward manifestation of inner sexual loathing, a symptom of internal rage and self-disgust. As Nicola points out, Marlow needs his illness as a weapon against others, using it 'as an excuse for not being properly human' (episode 6).

By the logic of this drama, to become a subject it is necessary to become masculine (masculinity and femininity not being equated here with biological maleness or femaleness). To become masculine, however, is to reject the feminine within oneself – femininity being culturally synonymous with passivity and dependence. Furthermore, in order to live his life, Marlow needs to divest himself of his unconscious and incapacitating sexual fear of women. As in Hélène Cixous's reading of the Oedipus story, the beast-woman has to be eliminated before Oedipus can become King.[37]

On a symbolic level the riddle of the sphinx must be solved before Marlow can proceed from the position of horizontal infant to upright man. The first stage of his hospital life is infantile dependency, the second is learning to stand upright, the third is the departure on the arm of his wife, whom he recognises not as an enemy but a support. To atone for the death of his mother, Marlow creates the singing detective as a super-ego, the radical reinvention of himself. Whereas Marlow is immobilised through his illness, his fictive alter-ego enjoys unrestricted mobility. It is the necessity to atone for Nicola's fictional death which impels Marlowe's release from the world of fantasy. Thus the recovery of the corpse from the water, ritually purified and cleansed, allows Marlow to rebuild himself and to gain self-love. It is through this mourning for the dead woman that Marlow can become whole again:

For the purpose of mourning is to kill the dead by ceasing to reanimate psychically a body physically absent; by withdrawing one's libidinal investment in a lost love object, forgetting or preserving it as dead. While the solution of the detective plot is to kill the 'dead' woman twice by virtue of deciphering and affixing a truth to her duplicitous body, the solution of the successful mourning plot is to kill the dead woman psychically preserved as a phantom, by virtue of decathesis. The solution of death that both detection and mourning provide in part serves to avert the idea that the death of another in fact threateningly signifies the presence of death in oneself.[38]

The dénouement takes the form of a 'shoot-out' between the singing detective he has created and the writer, Philip Marlow. In the gun-fight it is the weak, debilitated element of his character which is killed off, allowing only the masculine aspect of himself to emerge, in a corrective remaking of the old self. It is only after he has been able to accept his wife for what she is, a friend and not a foe, that full psychic recovery has become possible. Marlow walks out of the ward in the Chandleresque garb of the detective whose hat and raincoat symbolise the successful assimilation of the superego into his reintegrated psyche. The drama ends with the boy suspended in the high tree-tops. The boyhood dream ('I be going to be – a detective') of becoming an investigator so he could impose his order and authority upon the disturbing world of women's sexuality ('everything ool be all right') (chapter 2) has come true.

1. I am indebted to my colleague, Nigel Wheale, for helpful criticism of this essay, and to students in my Late Twentieth-Century Literary Culture Seminar at Anglia Polytechnic University, with whom the ideas in this essay were first discussed.
2. John Naughton, 'Potent Clichés and Painful Truths', *The Observer Review*, June 12, 1994, p. 5.
3. Peter Lennon, 'Dennis Potter: A Man With a Lash', *The Listener*, November 20, 1986, pp. 14-15, p. 15.
4. The name 'Marlow' is deliberately spelt differently from the character in Raymond Chandler's work.
5. Christopher Dunkley, *The Financial Times*, November 12, 1986, p. 23.
6. 'One of the things I want to do in The Singing Detective is break up the narrative tyranny.' Dennis Potter, quoted in Philip Oakes, 'A Suitable Sleuth for Treatment', *The Radio Times*, November 15-21, 1986, p. 98.

7. Rosalind Coward, 'Dennis Potter and the Question of the Television Author', *Critical Quarterly,* vol. 29, no. 4, p. 83.
8. 'Dennis Potter', unsigned obituary, *The Times,* June 8, 1994, p. 8.
9. Paul Giles, 'History with Holes: Channel Four Television Films of the 1980s', in Lester Friedman (ed.), *British Cinema and Thatcherism: Fires Were Started.* London: UCL Press, 1993, p. 71.
10. ibid.
11. Lester Friedman, preface to *British Cinema and Thatcherism*, p. xix.
12. Interview with Melvyn Bragg, broadcast Channel 4, April 5, 1994, reproduced in *New Left Review*, no. 205, May-June 1994, p. 134, p. 138.
13. John R. Cook, *Dennis Potter: A Life on Screen.* Manchester: University Press, 1995, p. 280.
14. Graham Fuller, (ed.). *Potter on Potter.* London: Faber & Faber, 1993, p. 133.
15. W. Stephen Gilbert. *Fight & Kick & Bite: The Life and Work of Dennis Potter.* London: Hodder and Stoughton, 1995, p. 169.
16. Peter Stead, *Dennis Potter.* Bridgend: Seren Books, p. 124.
17. T. Carrigan, B. Connell and J. Lee. Hard and Heavy: Towards a New Sociology of Masculinity', in M. Kaufman (ed.). *Beyond Patriarchy: Essays by Men on Pleasure, Power and Change.* Toronto: Oxford University Press, 1987, p. 179. Quoted in Robert Hanke, 'Redesigning Men: Hegemonic Masculinity in Transition', in Steve Craig (ed.), *Men, Masculinity, and the Media.* Newbury Park and London: Sage 1992, p. 190.
18. ibid.
19. ibid., p. 196.
20. Andy Metcalf and Martin Humphries. *The Sexuality of Men.* London: Pluto Press, 1985, p. 14.
21. ibid., p. 6.
22. Joost Hunnigher. 'The Singing Detective (Dennis Potter): Who Done It?', in George W. Brandt (ed.). *British Television Drama in the 1980s* Cambridge: University Press, 1990, pp. 234-57.
23. Melvyn Bragg interview, op. cit., p. 136.
24. Kaja Silverman, 'Historical Trauma and Male Subjectivity', in E. Ann Kaplan (ed.). *Psychoanalysis and Cinema.* London: Routledge, 1990, p. 114.
25. Nicole Ward Jouve, *The Streetcleaner: The Yorkshire Ripper Case on Trial.* London: Marion Boyars, 1988, p. 51.
26. Richard Dyer, 'Don't Look Now: The Male Pin-Up', in *Screen* (eds.). *The Sexual Subject: A Screen Reader in Sexuality.* London: Routledge, 1992, p. 267.
27. Melvyn Bragg Interview, op. cit., p. 135.
28. John Ellis, 'Prologue: Masculinity as Spectacle: Reflections on Men and Mainstream Cinema', in Steven Cohan and Ina Rae Hark (eds.). *Screening the Male: Exploring Masculinities in Hollywood Cinema.* London: Routledge, 1993, p. 17.
29. Elisabeth Bronfen, *Over Her Dead Body: Death, Femininity and the Aesthetic.* Manchester: University Press, 1992, p. 153.
30. Frank Krutnik, *In a Lonely Street: Film Noir, Genre, Masculinity.* London: Routledge, 1991, p. 52.
31. Mary Ann Doane, *Femmes Fatales: Feminism, Film Theory and Psychoanalysis.* London: Routledge, 1991, p. 1.
32. Wendy Hollway, 'I Just Wanted to Kill a Woman' Why? The Ripper and Male Sexuality', in *Feminist Review* (eds.). *Sexuality: A Reader.* London: Virago, 1987, p. 131.
33. See Graham Fuller, op. cit., p. 133.
34. Sigmund Freud, 'On the Universal Tendency to Debasement in the Sphere of Love' (1912)', in The Standard Edition of *The Complete Psychological Works of Sigmund Freud.* London: Hogarth Press, 1961, vol. xi, pp. 177-91.
35. Jane Selvege, 'We're No Angels – Images of Nurses', in Kath Davies, Julienne Dickey and Teresa Stratford, (eds.). *Out of Focus: Writings on Women and the Media.* London, The Women's Press, 1987, p. 198.
36. ibid., p. 199.
37. Hélène Cixous, 'Castration or Decapitation', *Signs* 7, 1981, pp. 41-53.
38. Elisabeth Bronfen, op. cit., p. 295.

Domesticating the Detective

Morag Shiach

What I will address in this article is a particular, one might even say peculiar, aspect of recent British feminist detective fiction. I want to explore some issues which arise from the narrative and symbolic importance of the female detective's male sexual partner and their domestic arrangements in novels by Val McDermid, Sarah Dunant, Michelle Spring and Gillian Slovo.

I am aware that feminist detective fiction is a difficult object for textual critics. Critical writing about feminist detective fiction so often amounts to a catalogue of disappointments, where the critic expresses frustration and anger at the failure of a range of texts to express or develop a coherent and effective version of feminist subjectivity.[1] Feminist detective fiction seems to disappoint its critics in a number of ways: by relying on liberal versions of individual agency; by portraying female detectives as amateur, as taking on cases only for family and friends rather than seeing themselves fully as players in the public world of crime; by failing to sustain the (fantasy of) autonomy for its female protagonists. Finally the genre seems to risk disappointing because its need for formal resolution creates a reactionary tendency to reinforce the status quo.

To understand the force of these criticisms, and to avoid simply restaging them, it is important to consider the historical emergence of feminist detective fiction in Britain in the eighties, and its relation to the feminist movement. The texts within this sub-genre share the following characteristics: they have a female detective; they 'challenge the gender norms of detective fiction';[2] they engage broadly with aspects of women's social position; they investigate the institutional and personal bases of oppression; and they also market themselves in relation to the sub-genre, either under imprints such as Virago or The Women's Press, or through publishing blurb which stresses terms such as 'fearless', 'feisty' or 'unconventional'.

Suggestions concerning the emergence of the sub-genre tend to connect it rather generally to political and cultural manifestations of the women's movement, including the Equal Pay Act or the Sex Discrimination Acts,[3] and in this sense to see feminist detective fiction as reflective of the emergence of cultural critiques of gender relations and of the modification of gender relations at work and in the home. What such accounts fail to address, however, is why detective fiction might be a particularly appropriate cultural form for the exploration of such transformations.

The emergence of detective fiction as a genre in the 19th century has been widely theorised. Walter Benjamin reads the genre in relation to the experience of the urban.[4] He sees detection as an expression of the fear of anonymity in the urban crowd. In the minute attention to detail, the forging of connections, the interpretation of individual dress, habits or speech, Benjamin argues that the detective story is both reflecting and alleviating social anxieties. This point is developed by Carlo Ginsburg, when he explores the relation between the methodology of a detective such as Holmes and late-19th-century developments in techniques of medical inquiry or in forms of social theory.[5] In each field he sees a tendency to privilege the minute detail, the unconscious or the ephemeral as revealing greater truths than can be understood by totalising systems of knowledge. Gillian Beer stresses the anxiety about origins which dominated scientific and cultural discourses of the 19th century and argues that detective narrative emerged as a cultural response to the unsettling and fearful experience of living with a vastly extended sense of historical and evolutionary time.[6] In Beer's account, the crucial aspect of detective fiction lies in its capacity to posit an origin for the action of its story, an event which grounds its narrative and which can be resolved. As one of Wilkie Collins's detectives says, the problem is to be 'sure of beginning far enough back':[7] to identify the salient aspects of a narrative which has a definite shape and a series of comprehensible causal connections.

All of these theorisations see detective fiction as a response to, or as an expression of, the social relations of modernity. If we see the women's movement as part of the history of modernity, with the struggle for women's suffrage emerging at the same historical period as the genre of detective fiction, we might expect to find something in these theoretical models to illuminate more precisely the emergence of feminist detective fiction as a sub-genre.

The fear of anonymity has particular resonances with the social and cultural roles and experiences of women, who for so long lost their property as well as their names on marriage and who always had a more difficult relation to the forms of public identity available on the streets of the modern city. One response to this loss of individual selfhood has been the construction of collective forms of identity, signalled through choice of dress or of political badge: this was as true of the suffrage movement as it was of feminism in the seventies or eighties. Feminist detective fiction dwells crucially on habits of dress, on the details of the detective's house, her musical taste, her leisure pursuits. These all enable the reader to construct a sense of shared identity through style. The threat of anonymity is lessened by the staging of the marks of a collective sense of urban style.

Beer's argument can also illuminate aspects of feminist detective fiction. Her interest was in the sense of futility and fear generated by the experience of the vastness of an evolutionary time-scale in the 19th century, but eighties feminists too were grappling with the vastness of historical categories, particularly with the longevity and the pervasiveness of the category of 'patriarchy'. The containable, and resolvable, struggles staged in detective fiction thus had a powerful appeal.

To capture the intensity and impossibility of readers' investments in feminist detective fiction, however, it is necessary to turn to a theorisation that addresses the role of detective fiction within postmodern culture. Fredric Jameson's analysis of Chandler's work evokes many terms that will be central to his subsequent theorisation of the culture of postmodernity, including fragmentation, socially distinct urban spaces and pastiche. The term which is most revealing in relation to feminist detective fiction, however, is nostalgia. Jameson argues that enthusiasm for Chandler 'is generally characterised by an attachment to a moment of the past wholly different from our own which offers a more complete kind of relief from the present'.[8] In her study of feminist detective fiction, Sally Munt notes that it emerges in a moment of crisis for the Left and for the organised women's movement, observing that 'certainly feminists of the 1980s spent more time reading than marching'.[9] This gap between the staging and resolution of problems in the fiction and the experience of political fragmentation and powerlessness may go some way to explain both the fascinations of the sub-genre and the disappointment that these novels seem always to provoke. Feminist detective fiction is perhaps always a poor substitute, addressing a community already nostalgic about the possibilities of effective collective identities.

The readers of feminist detective fiction, including myself, bring impossibly contradictory fantasies to the reading of these texts: they seek a narrative of effective autonomy and a sense of community but also are committed to replaying the elegiac recognition of the failures of feminist collectivities. In addressing my own disappointments about the representation of the detectives' sexual partners in a number of novels, I am not suggesting that these novels could or should have done things differently but rather I am trying to understand the reasons for a particular imaginative redundancy concerning issues of the domestic.

The detective and the domestic have long been in tension. Sherlock Holmes's domestic arrangements are both unusual and impersonal, while Dupin's preferences are for isolation and darkness and he chooses to live in a house which is 'long deserted through superstitions into which we did not inquire'.[10] Raymond Chandler was clear about the antithesis between detection and the domestic, insisting that 'a really good detective never gets married', while Dorothy L. Sayers suggested that 'the less love in a detective story the better'.[11] Chandler's objection is not the same as Sayers's: he sees marriage as disturbing the fantasy of the detective's autonomy and self-reliance, while Sayers fears that love interest might move a story from the realm of detective fiction into the merely novelistic. Nonetheless, marriage and sustained emotional and sexual relations are both seen as barriers to the construction of a true detective narrative. One might expect the writers of feminist detective fiction to heed such warnings, both because it is notoriously difficult to create narratives of romance or of the erotic which do not simply repeat existing power imbalances, and because the domestic has been a space of confinement and containment for women socially, economically and imaginatively. We might therefore conclude that a form of fiction which explores female agency in the realm of the public might be likely to avoid the domestic and its entanglements.

In fact, the novels I will explore insist on constructing a domestic space and identity for their female detectives, though they rather carefully avoid marriage. The texts themselves acknowledge this departure from the classic detective tradition. Sarah Dunant has her heroine, Hannah Wolfe, remark:

> At the foot of the bed the TV was droning on quietly, yet another detective drama, the lone hero putting the world to rights while his own internal landscape fell apart. I knew how he felt.[12]

Since the remark is made while Hannah is being comforted by her lover, the identification with the lone detective is at best strained. Dunant, McDermid, Slovo and Spring do not want to abandon 'the internal landscape' and they do not want to catalogue a series of sexual conquests. Equally, they cannot risk the enclosure of the nuclear family. Their narrative solutions are strikingly similar, as the following quotations suggest:

> Richard was my lover next door, a funny, gentle divorcé with a five-year-old son in London.[13]

> This was Nick's Saturday for not having Josh and we had agreed to spend the evening together.[14]

> Sonny and I have always aimed for separate but parallel lives. A shared life during the week, when Dominic and Daniel are at their mother's. And lots of separate time around weekends and vacations, when Sonny fulfils his fatherly commitments and I hang out with my friends.[15]

Similarly, Gillian Slovo's heroine Kate Baeier has a lover called Sam, whose son Matthew is 'at his mother's in the week and Sam's at the weekend'.[16]

These male lovers share some crucial characteristics: they are divorced; not particularly successful in their careers nor particularly ambitious; and they are fathers of sons. They also share charm, infantilism and winning smiles:

> Richard Barclay, rock journalist and overgrown schoolboy. . .when he saw me his face lit up in my favourite cute smile.[17]

> He's a nice guy with a well-developed sense of humour.[18]

> The third, tall and lean with a smile that would melt your heart – did still after all these years melt mine – was Sonny.[19]

The repetition of these characteristics suggests that they do not simply emerge from particular plot demands, but that they address something quite fundamental about the constraints of feminist detective fiction as a genre. The figure of the divorced, chlidlike, dependable father of boys is overdetermined in these narratives. Firstly, these men allow the detective to be sexualised without threat. As divorced men they are sexually experienced, but also have demonstrated their capacity to establish committed and long-term relationships, even if these ultimately failed. In feminist theory and fiction, female sexuality is a crucial marker of power and of agency and the detective thus must be sexually knowledgeable and active. Sexual passion, however, risks disturbing the judgement and the control of the detective. Chandler, of course, ran this risk, but had his detective walk away from sexual desires and fantasies at the end of his novels. For Slovo, McDermid, Spring and Dunant, such a resolution is not possible, since they want to challenge the power and exploitation inherent in the fetishistic figure of the *femme fatale*. The uneasy solution lies in containing sexual passion within the bounds of the habitual and the humorous: less erotic than cuddly.

Secondly, these male figures offer no challenge to the narrative centrality of the detective: they are insufficiently interesting to do so. All the novelists thus heed Sayers's warning rather more rigorously than she did herself. It has been frequently observed that Sayers's female detective, Harriet Vane, is disabled by her passions and always resolves her cases with the authority and experience of Lord Peter Wimsey. Contemporary novelists do not want to risk such swamping of the female detective.

Thirdly, all of these novels evade the representation of the mother-daughter relationship and only hint in the most ironic terms at a maternal relationship between the detectives and their lovers' sons. The oedipal relationship is thus played out to the side of the female detective, who never has to confront the impossible social and cultural expectations of the mother as bearer of femininity.

Finally, these male characters and their episodic relations to their lovers allow the writers to displace conflicts in time, over power, autonomy and agency, into conflicts over space. The different flats and houses in these novels contain different forms of subjectivity, and separate the public and the private whose contradictions can thus be evaded. This separation is most clearly marked in McDermid's novels, where Kate Brannigan and her lover live in separate houses which are joined by a shared conservatory. The device certainly leaves the detective with more time and energy for detection, but also feels like an evasion of many of the issues concerning power and control to which these novel so insistently allude.

The representation of the male lovers in these novels seems, finally, remarkably safe for a genre that explores fear, conflict and danger, and a certain dissatisfaction with these figures is clear in the most recent works by the novelists I have been discussing. Thus, for example, having featured his arrest in *Crackdown* (1995), in *Blue Genes* (1996) McDermid stages the death of Richard Barclay. The death is fake, a plot device to enable Kate Brannigan to investigate fraud aimed at the newly bereaved, but the murderous intentions might nonetheless be real. Gillian Slovo sees these intentions through and kills off Kate Baeier's lover, Sam. In *Catnap* (1994), Kate has to come to terms with this death, which turns out to have been partly her fault, and also has to establish a sustainable relationship with Sam's son. In neither is she entirely successful, and she moves through the novel in a driven craze of anger, revenge and denial. But these developments do suggest that as fictional women detectives become increasingly assured in their negotiation of the public world of crime, they can be represented as less predictable, less contained, and perhaps as more fun in their construction of the domestic.

1. For examples of this 'disappointment' see Glenwood Irons (ed.). *Feminism in Women's Detective Fiction*. Toronto: University of Toronto Press, 1995.

2. Maggie Humm, 'Feminist Detective Fiction', in Clive Bloom (ed.). *Twentieth-Century Suspense*. London: Macmillan, 1990, p. 237.

3. See, for example, Nicola Nixon's article in *Feminism in Women's Detective Fiction*, 29-45.

4. Walter Benjamin. *Charles Baudelaire: A Lyric Poet in the Era of High Capitalism*. Trans. Harry Zohn. London: NLB, 1973, pp. 43-8.

5. Carlo Ginzburg. 'Morelli, Freud And Sherlock Holmes: Clues And Scientific Method.' *History Workshop* No. 9 (1980), 5-36.

6. Gillian Beer, ' Origins and Oblivion in Victorian Narrative', in *Arguing with the Past*. London: Routledge, 1989, p 12-33.

7. Wilkie Collins. *The Moonstone*. Oxford: Oxford University Press, 1982, p. 9.

8. Fredric Jameson, 'On Raymond Chandler', in Glen W. Most and William W. Stowe (eds.). *The Poetics of Murder: Detective Fiction and Literary Theory*. New York: Harcourt Brace Jovanovich, 1983, p. 135.

9. Sally R. Munt, *Murder By the Book?: Feminism and the Crime Novel*. London: Routledge, 1994, p. 27.

10. 'The Murders in the Rue Morgue', *The Complete Tales and Poems of Edgar Allan Poe*. Harmondsworth: Penguin, 1982, p. 144.

11. Raymond Chandler, 'Casual Notes on the Mystery Novel', in D. Gardiner and K. Sorley Walker (eds.). *Raymond Chandler Speaking*. London, 1962, p. 70. and Dorothy L. Sayers in Howard Haycroft (ed.). *The Art of the Mystery Story: A Collection of Critical Essays*. New York: Bilboo and Tanner, 1975, p. 104.

12. Sarah Dunant. *Fatlands*. Harmondsworth: Penguin, 1994, p. 67.

13. Val McDermid, *Dead Beat*. London: Victor Gollancz, 1992, p. 15.

14 . *Fatlands*, p. 40.

15. Michelle Spring. *Running for Shelter*. London: Orion, 1995, p. 6.

16. Gillian Slovo. *Death By Analysis*. London: The Women's Press, 1986, p. 48.

17. *Dead Beat*, pp. 11 and 71.

18. *Fatlands* p. 42.

19. *Running for Shelter*, p. 205.

Men, Women and the Law

Mavis Maclean

How does the legal framework which regulates family life deal with issues of gender? The thrust of post-war thinking towards equal rights for citizens regardless of ethnicity, gender and, more recently, age and sexual orientation, is embodied in fine-sounding international conventions. We struggle on in the UK as subjects of the Queen not citizens, without the protection of constitutional rights – a factor recently painfully apparent under the extremes of the Thatcher administration. But even here the European Convention on Human Rights is beginning to find application in our courts. Where there is a conflict between our own common law practices or statute-based law coming from Parliament, then the ECHR with its insistence on human rights and equality must now prevail. But is equality enough when dealing with the family lives of men and women? Do we seek more? If the playing field is unequal, is an impartial referee sufficient to ensure fair play, or do those running uphill need a start? Legal philosophy does have a mechanism for thinking about such issues and it can be a powerful tool. When talking about equality (as Americans, the UN and the ECHR do), all we need to do is move on from the rather simple notion of equality of opportunity, where the concern is to offer to everyone the same pathway, and to promote equality of outcome – i.e. to look to the end result. Then if equality of opportunity is not delivering the goods we can add ingredients to the package until it does.

Family law is a curious business. If we take the modern view of the family as a social system based on affective relationships, then the law seems to be attempting to regulate what is unregulatable. If we look back to the days when the family was a social system based on rights over land and legitimacy of succession to that property with accompanying duties to the crown under the feudal system of tenure, then the regulation of family life looks rather different. Indeed our family law has always lain close to our law of property, and this is what has determined its approach to men and women. The privacy of conception, the invisibility of biological fatherhood and the visibility of biological motherhood required strict control of the behaviour of the woman in order to ensure that the land passed to the rightful heir and was not diverted to the line of another man. Thus the need arose for visible signs and rituals to accompany the union of a man and woman which is intended to be the mechanism for producing heirs, with strict definitions of what is and is not a legitimate offspring, with rules of succession where there is no clear heir and rules for dealing with the case of men and women who cannot continue in their union. These usually involve some mechanism for living apart but rarely for the possibility of re-partnering, which may give rise to subsequent children and thus to disputed succession.

The Church provided a useful structure for legitimating such linear familial obligations and also the opportunity for highly visible rituals of marriage and christening the legitimate offspring, as well as providing the means of enforcement of the prescribed rules through fear of excommunication and damnation, which seem to have been rather more effective than a fine or a spell inside.

The legal structure was more concerned with social systems, from kingdom to family, than with individuals. The woman was the mother of her sons, and the daughter of her father, the mechanism for the transmission of property across generations. In a period when the time between generations was short, this was urgent business.

Regulation of family life now is far more focused on the role of the individual. Marriage is less regulated, and we have just acquired a law which will permit divorce basically on application with a waiting period, in the Family Law Act 1996. Our previous divorce law, though basing the divorce on the irretrievable breakdown of the marriage, retained an element of fault in that some of the ways of indicating that the marriage had broken down involved proving the unacceptable behaviour of the spouse, whether this involved adultery or cruelty. The right of the individual to seek a satisfactory partnership relationship and the right to leave a relationship which is not acceptable is now established. The claims of the family as an ongoing cross-generational institution are nowhere to be seen. Illegitimacy has gone from our legal system. We have testamentary freedom, unlike many of our European neighbours: the Englishwoman's right to leave her patrimony to a cat's home is sacred though mystifying to our European friends.

But how has the new emphasis on the individual affected women? I suggest we look closely.

I suggest that a woman may fare rather better when her role is seen as part of the seamless web of the ongoing family, when she is indispensable, when child-bearing is the primary requirement in a perilous world, and when her virtue and honour are beyond price. Such a view is heresy to any modern feminist but I put it forward at least half-seriously.

The child bearing if not the child rearing is not going to go away. Though early feminists, particularly in the US, managed to ignore it, they did so at their peril and now live without maternity benefit or job security or part-time job opportunities. If the child bearing will not go away even to a convenient test-tube of some kind, then does it make sense to base a legal system for the regulation of family rights and duties on the equality of individuals? Unless we can look to equality of outcome. . .

Let us take two examples. We have a divorce rate of one in three approaching one in two marriages. Arguments continue over whether this represents the economic power of women, newly acquired, which enables them to walk away from relationships which they find unsatisfactory. William J. Goode likens divorce to a luxury commodity: we can afford higher aspirations now, and the only problem is not to deal with the collapse of society as we know it but simply to find a way of managing the serial monogamy which follows. It is certainly true that in the UK three out of four divorce petitions are brought by women, but I have my doubts as to whether the women are ending the marriages. I suspect that they are in fact dealing with the practical effects of the ending of a marriage by seeking to sort out the financial aspect of the separation. It will be interesting to see whether the gender imbalance changes under the new legislation which will require couples to sort out their financial arrangements before a divorce decree is obtained, thus requiring the party who wishes to end the marriage to act.

There are two aspects of modern divorce law which highlight the perils for women of the individual citizen approach to family law. One is the question of joint custody, the second is the development of rules for the division of property.

1. Joint Custody

When a marriage ends and there are children what do we want the legal framework to say about responsibility for the children? In the UK the traditional mode of operation throughout the 20th century has been for children to live with their mothers. This was not always the case. At a time when a child represented an economic asset and would work rather than consume, or represented the heir to any property and by a process of transference took on the quality of a piece of property himself, then children were the property of their fathers. But since children have become economically inactive consumers, in need of nurture and care rather than being economically active and productive, their physical presence came to rest with the nurturing parent, i.e. the mother. The Children Act of 1989 changed all of this. Hereafter children were no longer to be seen as items of property to be disposed of with other assets after a divorce, but were to remain the responsibility of BOTH parents throughout their minority. Both parents were deemed to be responsible for the child and were now expected to make their own arrangements for the nurture of the child. Courts and lawyers were no longer to be drawn into making decisions about who should have this precious asset. In future parents were held to be responsible for their children and the role of the court was to be reduced to dealing with DISPUTE over specific practical matters, such as where a child was to live and who was to be in touch with that child either in person or by telephone or letter. This marked a major step forward in dealing with the thorny problem of moving from assuming custody to rest with either the mother or the father, through the murky prism of joint custody where both the parents were deemed to have decision-making powers over where he/she would live, which school he/she would attend, what medical interventions were appropriate, what religious practices should be observed and so on. At this stage the move towards parental equality of treatment had led in practice to shared control but responsibility for day-to-day support and care lay with the primary care giver, the resident parent, i.e. in nine cases out of ten the mother. The move to continuing parental responsibility marks a step forward in that the child is no longer treated in law as an item of property to be haggled over, but as an individual needing ongoing support; but in practice this excellently pragmatic piece of legislation recognises that the resident parent will normally make the relevant decisions, and the non-resident parent if he wants to challenge any of these will have to take the initiative in approaching lawyers and courts.

Thus the move away from talking about mothers and fathers to talking about parents was initially problematic for women, but by going beyond the theory of parental equality to dealing with the practical realities of where a child lives and who is the primary carer, we have emerged on the other side of this debate with the practical powers needed by the woman safely back in her hands.

2. Property

Here again we have the problem of apparent moves towards gender equality leading to difficulty in practice. What happens in the real world when in law we stop talking about support for wives and move into talking about spousal support and matrimonial property? Under the canon law of the Church, when a couple separated before the days of civil divorce *a mensa et thoro*, from bed and board, but were not actually released *a vinculo matrimonii* to marry again, the problem of the dependent female was dealt with by awarding to her a third of the man's income (leaving aside the question of property passing through her from her father to her sons). As the marriage continued the property remained with the husband to be passed on to the children of the marriage. A third of the income passed into the common-law set of expectations, quasi rules, about the way that a man should support a former spouse. Conduct played a part in determining entitlement to a share of the property of her marriage and to a continuing transfer of money, known as periodical payment, after the separation. But the interests of the children of the marriage came to dominate arguments about the way continuing support should be paid and the way that property should be divided. In the UK, as a common-law jurisdiction without codified rules, we have always been a little uncertain about the way any particular case would be decided if it came to court. This may in part explain the continuing serious role for lawyers in determining post-divorce financial arrangements (though the availability of legal aid is clearly a major factor also); but nevertheless we can trace a move away from a clear notion about what is due to a wife and the children. . . and a move towards the kinds of rules found in some American states, notably California, where a 50-50 property split became mandatory. As women became more economically active and more able to earn salaries commensurate with those of men, and as child support became separated from wife support and seen as a completely separate set of duties and entitlements, then the focus of post-divorce financial arrangements shifted towards dealing with property rather than ongoing or periodical payments. The clean break notion reached the peak of its popularity in the UK in the mid-1960s under the aegis of the Campaign for Justice in Divorce, a pressure group of divorced men and their second wives who argued persuasively for the 1984 legislation which promotes the clean break. Why should men continue to support ex-wives who often retained the children and, under the matrimonial jurisdiction which trumped property rights, the house also – even if only until the child reached its majority.

In practice, however, moving towards a 50-50 split and away from any ongoing payment to a former wife, has been severely damaging to the economic position of women. Such a division of property on the table fails to take into account the impact of child-bearing and primary caretaking on the earning capacity of women. This is particularly important to understand not only in relation to the current economic position but even more so in relation to the pension entitlement to come after retirement. If a woman accepts a 50-50 split of the property on the table at the end of the marriage she sells herself short with respect to the pension which will result from the marriage as a joint enterprise in which she took primary responsibility for child rearing on the understanding that although her pension rights would thereby be limited those of her partner would be unaffected and would be available to the pair on retirement. Again the approach of regarding both parties to a marriage as individuals requiring equal treatment before the law leaves the women seriously disadvantaged. Only recognition of the fact of motherhood and its economic impact can save a woman from financial problems after divorce – unless she repartners and acquires a second economically effective partner. And even here women are disadvantaged if this assumption is allowed to underpin pension-fund rules, for although men repartner at any age women are unlikely to do so after the age of 40.

Women, it seems, can only suffer from equal treatment under the law, in relation to the issues surrounding serial monogamy. Any attempt to produce real equality of outcome has to take into account the inequality of entry into the system, and this requires compensatory action and acknowledgement of the gender difference and impact of parenthood for women as primary caregivers.

Is the law a tool for achieving this kind of recognition? We must consider carefully what we want from the legal regulation of family matters. Do we seek a powerful tool for enforcing a particular moral or religious code? Probably not. Do we seek only a minimal level of protection for some from physical harm? If so could such a code be enforced under the criminal code? Maybe we seek more than this.

I suggest that we should seek to use the law to level the playing field before regulating the consequences of changing family forms, and in particular the new co-existence of serial monogamy and continuing or parallel parenting. The rhetoric of equality will not suffice unless it is clearly understood to be equality not only of opportunity but of OUTCOME.

In some countries the regulation of family matters has been strongly resisted as the family is seen as a private place in which the authority of the state may be resisted and other ways of social organisation can be explored. For example, in Eastern Europe the family was the only social organisation where honest communication could take place in an atmosphere of trust. But in the Western world, especially where feminist thinking is present, the family is seen as a locus of power and in such circumstances any withdrawal of legal intervention can only support the status quo, i.e. the survival of the strongest. If we see the family as a Hobbesian battleground, then the status quo is not good enough: the playing field must be levelled. This is the proper function of legal regulation in the interests of all weaker parties whether they be women, children or the elderly. The public/private distinction loses its validity when both the public and private spheres of activity are seen as dominated by similar power struggles; and here the first job of the law must be to support the weaker party. A family law which ignores gender differences will find this a daunting task, however unpalatable this recognition may be. One way around it is to focus on the parental relationship rather than the relationship between adult partners, as it is here that both physical and economic vulnerability arise. It also helps us to surmount the impact of concentrating on the legal institution of marriage when cohabitation is becoming more prevalent and salient every year. Perhaps the parental relationship is the best indicator of the presence of a vulnerable partner, as it is gender free in theory though not in practice and can deal with the needs of individual parents according to whether or not they take primary day-to-day responsibility or whether they are free to go and earn in the marketplace.

Further Reading

John Eekelaar. *Regulating Divorce*. Oxford University Press, 1994.
Colin Gibson. *Dissolving Wedlock*. London: Routledge, 1994.
Mavis Maclean. *Surviving Divorce*. Basingstoke: Macmillan, 1991.
Lenore Weitzman and Mavis Maclean. *The Economic Consequences of Divorce*. Oxford: Clarendon Press, 1992.